THE
NETWORK
MARKETING

SELF-STARTER

Incorporating the **100 DAYS PLAN**

– the ultimate answer to Networking

and M.L.M. success

Allen Carmichael

By the same author:
MULTI-LEVEL MARKETING ISBN 1 873288 0 X
First published by CONCEPT July 1990
Second edition published as 'NETWORK & MULTI-LEVEL MARKETING'
ISBN 1 873288 01 8
August 1991

ISBN 1–873288–02–6

Production and design by Dinah Parkinson
Cover design by Allen Carmichael

Typeset by Cambrian Typesetters, Frimley, Surrey.
Printed in Great Britain by Cox & Wyman Ltd, Reading, England.

CONTENTS

SECTION ONE – The route to success

SECTION TWO – Nuts and bolts

SECTION ONE
THE ROUTE TO SUCCESS

INTRODUCTION

I have been fortunate to have had the experience of looking at and sitting in on all manner of meetings, seminars, training sessions and general conversations concerned with Multi-Level or Network Marketing and I can't help feeling that a degree of standardization of the vocabulary involved in this industry might be a distinct advantage!

Whilst some people cling to 'Multi-Level Marketing', others favour 'Network Marketing' – both names for the same concept. Some favour 'recruiting' as opposed to 'sponsoring', others 'selling' as opposed to 'sharing'. There are, of course, subtle differences between, for example, recruiting and sponsoring. To recruit is merely to enlist whilst to sponsor does imply accepting a degree of responsibility for the person concerned. There are probably more variations than I have listed, but does it really matter? These are relatively minor points and do not affect one's understanding of the basic principles of this fascinating marketing method – or indeed the degree of success attainable through its practice and promotion.

The words we employ are of far less relevance or importance than what we actually do to enact the meaning of them. However, a vocabulary we must have, and a measure of agreement would probably be a help to universal understanding. In the context of this industry the responsibility is that of teaching – *and teaching to teach*. That, in essence, is what the whole thing is about, and once that concept has been grasped, you are on your way to success . . .

But it isn't actually *quite* as easy as that to many people – simply because that apparently straightforward idea seems to be a most difficult thing for them to take on board. The aim of my first book (Network & Multi-Level Marketing) was to provide a very simple introductory explanation of what Networking requires from the individual, and I used a number of diagrammatic illustrations to help in conveying the concept. It was aimed at the newcomer to the subject, to satisfy their curiosity and answer many of the basic questions. The book you are now reading is a companion to the first, picking up the themes and enlarging on them for the benefit of the person who, having become intrigued, wants to know more about the subject. It is designed to both motivate and inform, indeed to act almost as a personal training course.

It may be that our economic climate offers the perfect conditions for the development of Network Marketing. How many business opportunities can there be that promise the possibility of financial independence within a few short years? And how many where the capital outlay is negligible, the risks virtually non-existent and the opportunity is one that can be approached on a toe-in-the-water basis without giving up one's normal occupational earnings until success is assured?

Network Marketing can offer a second chance in life – and life doesn't offer second chances very often – to people hit by the devastating blow of redundancy or to others tired of the struggle to keep a business alive under the burden of high interest rates, spiralling wages and inescapable fixed overheads.

Perhaps all this sounds too good to be true . . .

Nobody plans to fail but many fail to plan! This corny old chestnut, like all the trite sayings that are often trotted out in motivational training, does contain the nub of a great fundamental truth.

People can fail in any business and people do fail in Network Marketing, often after having started out with tremendous initial enthusiasm. They were ready to conquer the world, eager to spread the message and reap all the rewards that they had been told Networking can offer. And yet, despite all that initial excitement, after a while they would fade away.

There are two clearly recognizable reasons for these failures. Either the people concerned were not doing what they had been taught, in the way they had been shown – there are always those who will try to reinvent the wheel – or they were suffering from lack of support. Possibly they had never sought it – or they were not offered it when it was most needed.

There are those – and there are very many of them – who haven't exactly failed but have never achieved the success they fervently believed would crown their endeavours. They failed to realize that the route to real and lasting success in Networking is to stick to one scheme or plan and to really work at it diligently.

Indeed, the plan this book embodies will point the way to ultimate success – but it will demand a 100% commitment from you – with all your energies concentrated on just one Network or MLM scheme, for that is the nature and essence of the plan. You cannot win a race by constantly changing horses. If you see your horse as a potential winner, put everything behind it, but above all, believe in it!

In the Networking industry, it is all too easy to adopt the 'green fields' mentality and allow oneself to be constantly distracted by the ballyhoo of each newly-launched scheme that promises immediate success with apparently no particular expenditure of effort.

Another trap into which it is easy to fall is to become a distributor to several Networking operations at the same time. All this achieves is to dissipate one's energies in such a way as to ensure that none of the schemes produces the promised rewards. Let me make it clear, in putting forward their ideas, I am not referring to all those people who run a 'Portfolio' of business opportunities as a planned and professionally managed operation. That is something quite different and I will have more to say on the subject of portfolios in Section Two. I am offering a warning to the newcomer – with no consistency of purpose, the rewards will *always* be disappointing. If this book can open the eyes of anyone who has fallen into this trap, and save them from becoming one of those lost souls, condemned, like the Flying Dutchman, to wander endlessly over a sea of opportunity without ever realizing what they must do to find true success, it will have achieved something really worthwhile!

There are many extravagant claims made in this industry – many of them greatly exaggerated, often mere myth – regarding the creation of astronomic numbers of millionaires and so on. There is no doubt about it, a lot of people have made, and are making, a lot of money in Networking. These, clearly, are *not* the people scratching around the edges . . .

To produce wealthy people in such numbers does imply that there must be a common denominator to their success – there is, for success and achievement of this calibre are certainly not the result of some kind of magic or luck. All these people understand that persistency, hard work, and above all, *belief*, are the three elements that go to produce that elusive thing called success.

When a new President is elected in the United States of America, or, nearer home, we acquire a new Prime Minister, the media have developed the practice of assessing progress and effectiveness on the basis of the 'first hundred days' in office. In Network Marketing and MLM there are undoubtably plans based on a greater or lesser number of days, but I felt that a hundred days was a reasonable and acceptable yardstick to adopt – a time by which anyone or any thing, after serious, consistent and single-minded effort, should be showing some sort of form – and seeing the beginnings of the related rewards.

So, that is what the '100 DAYS PLAN' is all about! There is no magic, no luck – just a simple plan based on consistency of effort but, with the added requisite of *knowing what you are doing, and why!* If you are willing to accept what Network Marketing is *as well as what it isn't*, YOU could join that happy band of high-achieving earners – some of whom *have* become millionaires – or at worst achieve financial independence.

Multi-Level or Network Marketing is not about selling skills, it is about people and the skills needed to understand and motivate them towards personal and collective success and achievement.

Success is not a point at which one suddenly arrives, it is a journey. The purpose of this book is to accompany you on that journey to make the way as painless as possible and to give you a definite route to follow. This is not the easiest business – but it is *simple*. Once you come to terms with that it *becomes* easy and there is no reason why you should not enjoy the exciting rewards that many have found to be the benefits of a career in Network Marketing.

Allen Carmichael, September 1991

QUESTIONS AND ANSWERS – AN EXPLANATION

What do you feel about your future?

Does your present job have the potential to alter it in any way?

What, indeed, would you ask of that future?

If you could start again, what would you change?

Do you have ideals and dreams? Where would you like to live? What car would you like to drive? Have you achieved your ideal life-style?

Would you like financial independence, more free time to explore the things that really interest you, more time to spend with your family and friends?

Would you like to feel that you were rewarded in direct ratio to the amount of effort you put into your work?

Everyone has dreams . . . but how near has the reality of your life so far come to those dreams? It is quite likely you have been asking yourself questions of this nature, otherwise you probably wouldn't be holding this book in your hands right now!

More than likely somebody has told you about Network or Multi-Level Marketing – or about some particular Network/MLM organisation. You may have heard extravagant stories and been quoted startling statistics about the number of people who have made their fortune through Networking. Possibly you have recognised Network Marketing as the opportunity you have been seeking – that 'something' that could eventually release you from the likelihood of a predictable future.

More and more manufacturers and providers of services are turning towards Network Marketing because it provides a viable alternative answer to cost-effective distribution. The use of Networking virtually dispenses with the need for expensive advertising since the product is publicized by word of mouth and by example – the individual being seen to use and believe in the product. This is the most effective form of 'advertising' from which any product could benefit.

In a world where rents, rates and wages spiral upwards with tedious regularity, one can understand how cost-containment must be the ever-present spectre for the manufacturer. Networking represents a very acceptable marketing alternative since markets develop and expand through the natural generic growth which is the basis of the idea. From the customer's viewpoint too, Networking is very acceptable; shopping in the comfort and privacy of your own home has a certain attraction to many people, and a natural development – the 'party-plan' – is one of the biggest growth areas within the industry. Direct sales generally are gaining ground all the time possibly because of the element of personal contact and service that is essential to the exercise. Sales are very easily generated in a group domestic environment since the social aspect creates a relaxed atmosphere and is a great stimulus to spur-of-the-moment buying.

Could it be that in the face of this revolution, shops, as we know them, might eventually disappear as more and more goods flow through the community on a tide of Multi-Level and Network Marketing? Scarcely a week passes without at least one announcement of a new plan. To the individual considering getting involved, Networking represents something quite unique in business opportunity since it is possible to start what may eventually become a business of startling proportions with next to no capital. The greatest asset you could possess is the ability to speak to people easily. Meeting people with ease and in a relaxed manner builds enormous confidence and gives you the credibility you need if you are going to interest them both in your product and in the opportunity you are able to offer. There is probably no other type of business that can offer such potential – yet sometimes this can be a difficult idea to accept since its very simplicity can give rise to doubts as to its effectiveness.

It is perfectly understandable that, on encountering Networking for the very first time, the conventional salesman often cannot comprehend what he is looking at. Who does the selling? To this man the notion of large numbers of people distributing modest amounts of product is difficult to accept. Once he understands that volume business comes through the multiplication that produces an ever expanding network, and that

11

sharing the business opportunity implies more and more product being distributed, he is on his way to greater earnings than his conventional activity could ever produce.

From the manufacturer's point of view, when it comes to the marketing of his product, his obvious wish and intent is to dispose of as many units of product by the easiest and most cost-efficient route he can devise. Conventionally he could follow the accepted method of selling his goods to a wholesaler, or several wholesalers, in bulk. The wholesaler then breaks down this large package into a number of smaller packages and distributes them to a number of retailers. The retailer breaks down his package into its individual components, displays them on his shelves and sells them, item by item, to his customers. As the product passes through each of these stages, the price rises as each operative in the chain takes his profit in recognition of his role in the distributive system.

As many as three or four people may be making a living by taking their profit as the goods pass briefly through their hands.

Let us assume that the eventual customer is satisfied with the price he pays for the product he has purchased. But would he feel quite so pleased if he knew what the unit cost of the product was as it left the factory?!

So, you may ask, why cannot the consumer buy direct from the manufacturer. There are several good reasons:

1. Many people needing the product would be

too far from the manufacturer to visit him to make their purchase.

2. The manufacturer uses all his energy in producing the product and may not have, nor indeed want to employ, the staff it would take to provide over-the-counter sales.

3. His volume of sales would be limited severely by the localized aspect of the operation.

4. The product could, of course, be sold by post but that would require a substantial outlay on advertising and publicity material. Of course, many sucessful businesses do operate in the Mail Order field, selling direct from the factory to the consumer. Such businesses rely on sophisticated systems, and carry very high postal and packaging costs which all tend to make the product more expensive to the customer. Nevertheless, this in no way invalidates the idea.

The manufacturer realizes only too well that the only way he can sell his product in sufficient volume to create financial viability is to make it available on the doorstep of his potential customers – and that they will only be aware of his product through the familiarity created by advertising. If the product is one that all households need and use regularly, the manufacturer will be faced with considerable competition from the stores whose shelves carry a whole range of similar products to his.

All this, of course, is amazingly costly and every on-going expense has to be added to the price of the product, the poor old consumer being the loser.

Anyone who knows anything about advertising

knows the value of the unpaid-for written word. A few lines of editorial exposure in a magazine or newspaper is usually worth far more than the cost of any advertisement. The whole world of public relations is based on the notion that if enough people see enough of the product, be it a manufactured item, a person, book, film or whatever, something will rub off and sales or success will result. The value of any form of personal recommendation cannot be underestimated, whether it be the written word, the spoken word or simply through example where the product is *seen* to be used.

It is for all these reasons that more and more manufacturers and providers of services are turning towards Network Marketing as an ideal method of distribution. Networking virtually dispenses with the need for advertising since the product is publicized by word of mouth and by example – the strongest forms of 'advertising'.

So, where do the advantages to the consumer lie? If the need for advertising has been removed and two or three levels of profit-taking middle men have been dispensed with, the product should be a great deal cheaper. The resultant saving through the simplification of the distributive chain can be applied to the general benefit of the whole system in other ways.

More cash can be made available for product research and development, the end result of which should be to provide a better product than that of its competitors which is being marketed through the 'normal' channels. Secondly, there will be money available to be spent in developing a network of commission-earners willing to share the opportunity and the product to eventually provide it with a far wider buying public than it might otherwise have enjoyed.

NOTE: See also Section II – Theme and Variations

THE
MULTIPLICATION

Supposing I employed you for 21 days and offered you the alternative of either being paid £25 a day or being paid 1p for the first day's work, and thereafter doubling up so that on day 2 you get 2p, day 3 you get 4p and so on – which method of payment would you choose?

If you opted for the first, you would be very foolish indeed! By that conventional method you would receive £525 for your 21 days work. By the multiplication method your pay would be £10,485.76 for the same period and the same effort!

This rather startling situation is only brought about by a matter of simple, compounding multiplication. Multiplication of this sort can produce truly startling results.

As I write I look out from my window on a green hill about a mile away. What makes it look green? The grass, yes! But stop to consider *how* the colour of that green hillside actually comes about. If the hillside was just bare earth and there was one single blade of grass growing there, I couldn't possible see it . . or could I? It seems to me that I *must* be able to see it, otherwise, when the hill is *covered* in single blades of grass, how do I perceive it as green? The appearance of green only comes about through the process of light reflecting off each individual blade and the overall effect is nothing more than that process through astronomic multiplication resulting in the smooth, even, overall green colour that pleases my eye.

So, there is a magic about multiplication that, to a large extent governs our lives, and if we were to apply the same principles to the selling of goods or services, how very beneficial it would be!

Imagine yourself with an excellent product to sell – a product which represents both quality and value for money and has a virtually limitless market as its potential. You are able to purchase the product direct from the manufacturer, for which you pay a wholesale price. You sell to your customers at the retail price and the difference naturally represents your profit.

Supposing, working 10 hours a day, 5 days a week, you are able to sell 20 units a week. In a 48 week year your sales amount to 960 units. The market is enormous but, no matter how hard you work, selling 20 units a week is all you can physically manage.

Then you have a bright idea! All your customers are delighted with the product and have shown a willingness to tell their friends about it; so you suggest to the five most ambitious amongst them that they could buy the product from you and *sell* it to their friends, thus creating a retail business of their own. Of course you are still a retailer since you maintain your profits on personal sales, exactly as before. The significant difference now, though, is that you have also become a wholesaler, recognizing the potential of what you are doing you can now set yourself a goal of selling just 10 units a week so as to have time to devote to the building of your Network. In the short term you have actually reduced your sales target.

Because you are good at your job you are able to train your five people to a point where, mainly on a part-time basis, they average 5 sales a week each. Your small group is now selling 35 units (your 10 plus 5 × 5) a week. The manufacturer of the product is very happy to pay you a volume bonus on the total number of units sold by your group, and your five new retailers are happy with the profits they are making – *until you persuade them that they could be doing the same thing you have done!* So they each go forth and recruit five people of their own. The group has now expanded to 31 people including you! And the weekly sales volume – once the 25 new retailers are trained – has increased to 160 units. You are earning your bonus commission on the volume sales of the whole network as well as the retailers profit on your own sales – but, because of the number of people you have recruited (or helped to recruit) and developed, the profit margin has been enhanced in recognition of your new status.

If you remember, 20 sales a week was all you could originally manage – and yet now you are responsible for the movement of 160 units in the same period. It doesn't take a lot of imagination to see where this can lead as the multiplication ploughs on under your guidance and supervision . . .

YOU

Level two	5 people	= 6 total	(35 units sold)
Level three	25	= 31	(160 units sold)
Level four	125	= 156	(785 units sold)
Level five	625	= 781	(3910 units sold)

If everything had worked properly and everyone maintained the production levels laid down above, your network would now be moving 3910 units per week! That is the equivalent of 187,680 units sold in a 48 week year against your original personal best possible of 960. The difference is between being content with a modest but reasonable income that has to be rebuilt each year, or becoming quite seriously rich with an income that will go on increasing and will continue on indefinitely. What a very difficult choice!

Perhaps it is easier now to understand why the hot-shot conventional salesman finds Networking a concept with which it is difficult to come to terms. The idea of prospering through *decreasing* your personal sales goes very much against the grain!

As you can see, success depends on involvement with others. People cannot work and flourish in isolation. In Network Marketing – an activity requiring a very high degree of motivation – the support, recognition and encouragement of others is essential. There is simply no substitute for constant contact with other people doing the same thing and encountering the same problems, and, even better, with people who have already achieved some degree of success.

And so, that is a simplistic explanation of what Network Marketing is all about. All that is required to make it work, and for the individual to prosper, is the right attitude of mind – and *that* is the purpose of this book. By the end of the '100 DAYS' you will be benefiting from a very realistic income – providing you have applied yourself to all the principles the plan imposes and have stuck to the rule of active development within one plan only.

I don't want to give you the idea that you should be too 'blinkered' in your approach. The development of a network can be quite a creative thing, and, in that context, one should always be prepared to exploit the unexpected or the accidental – anything, in fact, that might help to speed up the end result. I remember watching a most extraordinary performance of completely blinkered behaviour on a farm in Sussex. A fox was crossing a hillside when a Jack Russell picked up its scent and began to follow it. The two animals crossed and recrossed the hill in lines that repeatedly took them within a few yards of one another. The fox, I suspect, must have been well aware of the fanatical dedication of the dog to the use of its nose, being totally intent, as it was, on following *scent* when *sight* would have short-circuited the chase and ended it dramatically!

Use this book as your training manual. Give it to others who are showing interest and let them discover the way to a whole new lifestyle – and possibly prosperity on a scale they had never considered likely.

Thoroughly learn the principles behind Networking. Learn so that you can pass on all this vital information easily and with authority to the people who will become a part of your expanding Network and your personal success.

THE INVESTMENT

Let's now examine what Networking requires of the individual – what sort of investment the '100 DAYS' of really active involvement will require.

1. *Money* – there will, of course be the outlay of a nominal sum of money. This is your stake in a new business venture. Most Networking operations require a registration fee – usually a modest amount which, in many cases, is renewable on an annual basis. The most successful companies impose this as a requirement since it acts as a reaffirmation of the individual's original intent. The renewal fee is like an annual cull, weeding out the deadwood in the organization with the effect of sharpening up the operation and re-focussing on those who are really serious.

Another investment you should be prepared to make is some form of 'starter pack'. This will contain technical information, sales, training and motivational material, and indeed, everything you will need to begin your business.

The finances are not in any way a critical factor if you retain your full-time employment until you have developed your new business to a point where you could go full time.

2. *Time* is the greatest investment you must be prepared to make. Time is a curious element. We all

have exactly the same amount; some squander it, some never seem to have enough of it, others steal it. Time is yours to do with what you will. Each moment only comes round once so it is far too precious to waste. Nobody has the right to waste the time of others, and yet many do – and do it quite wantonly. Don't steal from others and don't let them steal from you. To make the proper use of time you must understand *planning* and we will go into this in more detail later. Suffice it to say, at this stage, that the time you spend in actively developing your business at the outset will be the greatest investment you will ever make. The time you put in has the ability to multiply, through the efforts of the people you train and teach into hundreds and even thousands of selling and recruiting hours – and this is the substance of the '100 DAYS' plan. Each day is vitally important. Just as human beings need goals to strive for, there is a fundamental need of achievement – to feel that at least *something* has made the day worthwhile. Each day only comes round once and there are only so many in each lifetime, so every one must be significant – and if you don't believe that, try missing one!

3. *Enthusiasm* – another vital investment. Watch other people, especially the very successful ones, and emulate their behaviour. Always be prepared to praise and encourage others for their accomplishments – and never think, because someone *is* successful, that they do not need your enthusiastic recognition – the most fundamental of all human needs. You will only understand the real value of this by experiencing praise

and recognition from others yourself.

These are the essential ingredients to all human endeavour. You cannot over-invest in enthusiasm, energy, or interest in your fellow human beings.

4. *Creativity.* You must become a creative entre-preneur! Look at what works for others, try every-thing, find what works for you. Approach problems as a creative exercise, and, in their solving you will find enrichment comes to your own life. Get help, give help, learn and teach. Consider this for a moment – imagination is the mother of creative thinking *but it can also be your greatest limitation* if it is allowed to run in the wrong direction.

5. *Hard work* and dedication to your goals. Everyone begins from the same point. You cannot buy your way in – if you are offered such an opportunity, examine it most carefully!

Networking is about people. People *seeking* and people *offering* opportunities, sharing business ideas and products. It is thinking about what *you* can achieve, then multiplying your effort through the efforts of others. It is a world in which everyone's prosperity depends on the prosperity of everyone else and because of this, broadly speaking, it generates all the most worthy human attributes and stimulates ambition in the individual. Anyone who comes into Network Marketing thinking it is about exploiting the efforts of others, is doomed, in the long term, to failure.

Speculate to accumulate, that is the message. The

more information and expertise you can invest in by understanding your product and the business plan used to market it, the more effective you will be. Be a sponge and soak up everything! Ask questions, seek answers – your success depends on it. You will soon discover how willing everyone is to help you and it is essential that you feel able to trust the person who introduced you into Networking as well as trusting the people up-stream of him or her – and they too must demonstrate both integrity and honesty. It is the credibility of the opportunity and of the individuals concerned that will maintain the *quality* of the developing Network.

DEVELOPMENT AND THE ACES IN THE PACK!

Since the purpose of this book is to point the way to the real rewards that Multi-Level or Network Marketing have to offer, we should be concentrating our attention on the solid companies with a really sound track record. The companies that have embraced Network Marketing completely and encourage their associates or operatives to build teams strong in both depth and width. I have already touched on the *matrix* opportunities, both the worthwhile opportunities as well as all those endless pre-launch, green-field, get-in-quick, be-in-at-the-start chances offering high rewards and rapid returns and yet almost in contradiction, are often surrounded by phrases like 'no outlay', 'no selling', 'no recruiting'. These are the schemes that indeed attract the get-rich-quick merchants who, somehow, never do seem to get rich either speedily or otherwise.

As someone wisely observed – *the trouble with opportunity is that it always comes disguised as hard work.*

The rewards in life come to you rather like throwing a ball into the air – it soars upwards, scribing the first half of a perfect parabola, reaches the pinnacle of its rise, then comes back to earth describing an exact replica of the curve through which it climbed. You receive from life, it seems, in direct proportion to your input – whether that be for good or otherwise.

Some people appear luckier than others but it is strange how often those people coincidentally just happen to be the ones that work the hardest! In the chapter on 'the multiplication' we developed a model of the Network concept – the principle, if you like. But what of the reality. Does the development always take place in the way we planned? Of course it doesn't! It is too much to expect that *everyone* is capable of the same production levels and the same recruiting activity. There will be drop-outs – that is inevitable. Networking has plenty of sparkling successes but it also has its fair share of failures; so that a yardstick is always available, we must always have a utopian model against which to assess both performance and progress.

In my book 'Network & Multi-Level Marketing' I developed the idea of what I then called 'Gold Bricks'. I hope I will be forgiven for repeating the general outline of this idea again here – though using a different imagery – since what it embodies is of considerable importance.

Instead of 'Gold Bricks' we are looking at what I intend to call 'the Aces in the pack'. In a pack of 52 cards there are only 4 Aces – in other words one for every 13 cards. In sponsoring or recruiting you are likely to bring people of varying value and capability into your developing network but, from time to time, a very special person suddenly appears – an Ace! The thing that distinguishes this person from other mortals in the pack is that he or she has an immediate and instinctive understanding of what Network Marketing is all about and is quick to take up the baton and really run with it. The life-blood of Network Marketing will always be new, fresh, enthusiastic people. Age or background have nothing to do with this. These are the people I now prefer to call the Aces in your pack – and it is they who will keep the development constantly motivated and revitalised.

Everything in life has both its positive and negative aspects – and there is a situation that can materialize in Networking which might be described as the 'opposite' to the idea of the Ace. Some people find that the effort needed to constantly motivate others is extremely tiring; the result can be that they themselves become dispirited and demotivated. De-motivation is easily sensed and can spread like a virus. A whole down-line can suffer when their motivational support has been withdrawn. The members of that down-line, denied the necessary stimulus, can very quickly lose interest and, at worst, drift away, until that carefully built leg of the development completely disintegrates. As you will quickly appreciate, it is extremely important that situations of this sort are identified very speedily – before any permanent damage can occur. Perhaps we should regard these people as the Jokers in our pack?

As you can see, it is also very important that you spot an Ace quickly so as to give him or her all the help and stimulus they need to expand their own operation with the minimum of delay.

There will inevitably be sections of your network that are quite sluggish in their development, but wherever an Ace appears, the sparks begin to fly and the pace suddenly quickens. These are the legs of your downline on which to expend all your energy so as to maximize the development of the network. Spend time developing the *right* people – those who are capable of making things happen.

I cannot impress upon you too strongly the importance of working as far down-line as you can go – even at times beyond the limitations of the levels that will produce your earnings. Motivation is *so* important – motivation and constant contact demonstrating recognition. This is what keeps people working and developing, driving their particular down-line leg deeper and deeper. Be alert to the possibility of an Ace appearing anywhere at any time and give him or her all the support and encouragement you possibly can. Follow these principles and retention – a serious problem with some organizations – will never be a problem for you. Don't let the Jokers get to work – but providing the necessary level of motivation is maintained, the Jokers won't stand much of a chance – some of them may even turn into Aces and the ones that cannot stand the pace may well drift away!

The network that started with you may not actually have developed along the lines you had originally planned, yet suddenly one part of it takes off like a forest fire – not because of you, perhaps, but because of this great asset, the Ace in the pack! You may of course be one yourself . . .

OPENING THE DOOR

Networking is capable of raising standards both of living and of human behaviour, developing people's natural or latent talents and creating wealth in a way that very few other enterprises could ever do. Just through its very nature, the help and encouragement it fosters enables many people to broaden their outlook and attain goals and, through that, a lifestyle they might not have thought possible. Network Marketing makes no promises and offers no guarantees – but by the very nature of things, guarantees usually imply constraint and restriction. The chance is there for all to seize.

The result of all this drive and energy must be to increase general wealth and social awareness and so eventually be responsible for the general enrichment of community life.

The newcomer to Networking is bound to be impressed by the feeling of energy and excitement that can be generated at an opportunity meeting, an event which will almost certainly be his or her first public encounter with this strange new world.

Let's look at the sequence of events that leads to the individual's successful entry into an MLM or Network Marketing operation.

1. Many people will have their first brush with

Networking as a customer but, as we have already seen, the likelihood is that some mention of the business opportunity will have found its way into the conversation, since the dedicated Networker finds it difficult to keep his excitement to himself and is always on the look-out for people who will listen to what he has to say!

You may like what you hear, show interest and, before you know it, your helpful sponsor will be scribbling diagrams and infecting you with his enthusiasm. You will almost certainly be invited to attend an opportunity meeting.

2. Opportunity meetings are exactly what their title suggests – and will normally be an introduction to the company and its product(s) and a presentation of the business and marketing plan that represents the opportunity on offer. There will usually be time for questions and answers, with the object, particularly, of satisfactorily dispelling doubts and worries about Pyramid Selling, market saturation and several other predictable questions which tend to appear at most meetings of this sort. Usually, after the close of the official meeting, people will naturally slide into a more relaxed and social mood. The person who sponsored you will want to know what you felt about the meeting. Say exactly what you think! A normal reaction on first encountering Network Marketing is one of scepticism. There will always be a number of people who didn't like or didn't appreciate what they heard. Network Marketing is not for everyone, and, indeed, it would not be *suitable* for everyone. If you have questions, ask

them. One of the surest 'buying signals' is the person who wants to ask a lot of questions. Theirs is an attitude clearly expressing considerable interest – but the all-important thing is that those questions are fully and frankly answered.

Those who have shown real interest and have obviously been intrigued by the content of the meeting will probably be lent a pack of material to take away with them. This will amplify what they have heard, providing more information about the products and marketing plan. The pack should also provide information on potential earnings, production bonuses and all the other important facts needed to put the opportunity into sharper perspective.

3. Within about 48 hours your sponsor will probably be in touch with you again, suggesting that you meet for a one-to-one meeting to answer further questions, clarify any baffling points, if necessary go over the business plan again – in fact, generally cement everything into place.

4. Although it might have occurred only fleetingly, there will almost certainly, somewhere along the line, have been mention of some form of capital payment. There is such variance in these matters that it is difficult to indicate what this might be precisely but, in the majority of cases, any outlay is unlikely to be more than about £50. You should regard this as your stake money. There are not, after all, many forms of new business that could be launched for such an amount!

However, should you be asked for much more than £50, do look very carefully at what is on offer. Weigh up all the pros and cons, ask a lot of questions and be sure you get full and candid answers. If you are told you must keep a stock of the product, make sure the company offers an agreement to buy back unsold items.

Do a little research locally and make your decisions based on these questions:

A. In your area, is there a likely market for the product?

B. What other similar products are available on the market?

C. Is the price right? Does it represent value for money? Is it competitive?

D. Does the price at which you will buy the product reflect a good profit margin when related to its selling price?

E. Does the product have an image with which you will be happy and comfortable?

F. Does the product have quality, viability and credibility – and will it appeal to most people and sell easily?

These are all wise considerations before making any definite commitment. When you feel totally satisfied – and don't let anyone hurry or harass you over your decision – pay your joining fee and prepare to get started.

But what is this fee for? Usually it is not without value as it will provide you with a 'starter pack' which should contain most of the 'tools' you will require to set you on the road. It is difficult to be more specific since these things vary so much from one company to another.

5. Next on your agenda comes training. This is one of the responsibilities of sponsorship. Now your sponsor has a vested interest in you and will be willing to help you in any way he or she can by teaching you about the product, and, more importantly making sure you have a complete understanding of the business and marketing plan and exactly how it works. By this time you will feel you are fairly familiar with this presentation – but what you must now face up to is the fact that *you* will be expected to learn this presentation well enough to be able to go out and show it to others, to the people you wish to sponsor at the start of your own network development.

Some organizations – generally speaking, the ones with more technical products – will have a training course for which a fee may be charged. Regard this as part of the investment you should be willing to make in the interests of your new career – *the one that could – if you do all the right things – bring you financial independence within a few short years!*

There are not many business opportunities in which the initial outlay required of the individual or the risk involved is negligible. There are virtually no overheads, no staffing requirement, no premises needed, no equipment or any of the usual costly outgoings associated with the setting up a business.

6. At this stage, let us assume that you are still an

employed person. You have every belief in the opportunity you have been exploring and have now committed yourself to it – but you still have to survive. It is perfectly easy to begin to work at your new business on a part-time basis, indeed, this is how most people come into the business. Giving say 10 hours a week to it will soon begin to show results as you sell both the product and present the business and marketing plan. You may only be talking to friends, family and people at your place of work but, slowly, your message will get through and results begin to appear. You will be adding to your normal employed income steadily, until you inevitably reach the point at which the possibility of *replacing it* is *reality!*

This really is the moment of truth!

You now have your *real* launch pad. You know that you can earn as much in Multi-Level or Network Marketing as in your past occupation, and you have carefully built a good foundation to your own network. Making the decision to go into it full time means that everything can only progress and develop faster. The world, at last, is your oyster! There are no limitations other than those you might impose on yourself, and it is, of course, from this point that the multiplication will make itself felt.

THE ROLE
OF SPONSOR

Why in Network Marketing do we more often speak of 'sponsoring' rather than 'recruiting'?

'Recruiting' is a very straightforward, commonly used word which everyone understands. It simply means enlisting. One might use it in the context of bringing someone into a scheme who was already in the business of Networking. The word 'sponsoring' has much broader and deeper implications. It is to do with responsibility and commitment. By sponsoring you are demonstrating to someone that you are going to help them in any way you can to get started in the business. You are going to teach them all you know but, even more importantly, you are accepting the responsibility to *teach them to teach*. You are going to help them with their own first sponsorships, since it is in your interests to supervise the development of the down-line that your activity has started.

Proper sponsoring is showing a committed professionalism and, unless it is carried out continuously, there will be no real success. The true rewards in networking come from the perpetual growth of your organization so that, like the root system of a healthy tree, there is an outward and downward spreading development bringing an ever-increasing flow of the essential nourishment that everything above requires for its survival.

We are not talking about get-rich-quick schemes. Far too many people tend to jump on the MLM/Network Marketing bandwagon hoping for a free ride. They do this with little or no idea of what the business is truly about so will inevitably become its eventual casualties – and every time this happens it tends to bring a measure of disrepute to the industy. Bad news can travel twice around the world before good news has come out of its front door!

Almost every family in Britain today feels the need for, and could certainly benefit from, additional income. Being hard-pressed is a purely relative thing. What may be riches to one person might represent hardship to another – it all depends on an established life-style and the responsibilities and commitments that surround it. For some, a few hundred pounds a month would make the difference between no holidays and having at least one a year – if not two! This book, if it has value, should be capable of helping to take you a step or two away from where you are now by pointing you in the direction you would like to take towards whatever happen to be your specific goals. Only you are capable of knowing where that is . . .

The sponsor's aim is *duplication*. True duplication doesn't come until your third level is in place – when the person you have sponsored has sponsored another.

Everything you do must be aimed at the duplication of your own effort. If you see yourself as a leader, your aim must be to duplicate yourself by developing others as leaders. If you haven't learned to duplicate, you are unlikely to succeed in any great way.

If your intention is – and it should be if you are ambitious – to build a highly successful business for yourself, you must be constantly on the look out for serious-minded people. The sort of people who think like you, people who have credibility, the all important factor when it comes to undertaking their own sponsoring. Take as your yardstick one simple question. Ask yourself, if they had approached *you*, would they have had sufficient credibility for you to accept them and listen to what they had to say? It has often been said that you only have one chance to make a first impression. Do, therefore, ensure that the people you sponsor are *right*. They are your standard bearers, representing your particular network. They must be able to bring credibility and status to the products or services you are presenting and sharing.

How does the opportunity to sponsor come about? It should ideally be as effortless as possible – the soft sell. Many chances will present themselves through the normal activities of your working life both in the development of your new Networking business and in the context of your full-time employment. Just talking to people in any easy and relaxing situation, people you may know well or people you have met casually and with whom you have slipped into a natural conversation. Meeting people can be a very enriching experience. It should be both enjoyable and easy – these are the circumstances that will give those you meet confidence in you. Image is very important – that first impression. People like meeting others they perceive as successful since success is something everyone respects and admires. Present the right image and you will have no difficulty in getting others to listen to you.

Middle to upper income group people are often very attracted to Network Marketing since they, being successful already, recognize the opportunity and are also quick to see and appreciate the benefits. Professional people too – usually their earnings depend very much upon their own efforts and expertise, so naturally, if they are ill or go away on holiday, earnings cease but overheads continue relentlessly. The idea of an extra source of income that goes on 24 hours a day, once it has been set in motion, is, to these people, very attractive indeed. These will very often turn out to be the Aces in our pack we talked of earlier.

Ideally then, it should never be difficult to put across your message, get people interested in both your product and your organization and the marketing plan that is used to build and maintain your network. Human beings, though, have a habit of asking questions and raising objections! These may be nothing more than 'closing signals', but – and this is of paramount importance – they *must* be answered with ease and authority – all part of the necessary confid-

ence-building. Questions do not represent a *threat*!
Treat them always as a genuine expression of interest.
That way they will always be easy to answer.*

* See also 'Objections' in Section II.

THE APPROACH

I cannot stress the point too strongly that your aim must always be *duplication* if you are seriously intending to develop a large and prosperous network. The search for new people must be continuous. The second most important task is to help others achieve their own sponsorships as this is all part of the process of adding depth to your organization.

It is not the sponsor's job to be *selective*. How can he or she determine who will and who will not be interested in the business opportunity on offer? The most unlikely people find their way into Network Marketing and any network will always contain a very varied cross section of humanity.

So, the rule of thumb should be that you, as a sponsor, talk to *anyone* and *everyone* about the opportunity and be prepared to show the business or marketing plan to all comers. There is bound to be a natural sifting and selection process continuously at work as more and more people are exposed to the opportunity. It will not appeal to everyone and only a certain number of the initial contacts you make are going to be receptive to the idea. Those whose enthusiasm you have aroused should be invited to an opportunity meeting without delay so that they may be exposed to the plan and to others, who, like themselves, are prepared to seriously consider the opportunity. Those to whom the plan does not appeal should, without doubt, become customers for your products!

It is almost impossible not to be selective *in some way*. Clearly there are certain people, in very general terms, who are particularly worth approaching, just as, inevitably, you cannot help ruling out certain others as totally unsuitable.

Human beings, being the predictably unpredictable creatures they are, will often show tremendous enthusiasm for an idea that is well presented but might, just as easily, soon lose interest and drop by the wayside. It is very likely that, to get the five really worthwhile people you want, you may have to sponsor fifteen to twenty. Don't spend a great deal of time on people you have to cajole or who need too much convincing to join. Such people are often lazy and will simply be a drain on your time and energy.

Enthusiasm is what we are seeking – people who are naturally motivated and excited by opportunity and adventure. They will respond to your attentions and appreciate your interest. People who are already successful are *always* worth approaching. They don't have to prove anything to themselves or anyone else and, having been successful in one area of life, stand a good chance of duplicating the experience in another. These people, as we have seen, are the Aces in our pack.

There is a very simple basic approach that can be used with almost anyone. Start by asking your prospect what they do for a living. The next casual question is 'do you enjoy your job?' You can only get a YES or a NO to this – with the possibility of a few colourful embellishments! If the answer is YES, ask 'do you see yourself involved in this job for the rest of your life?' Very few people indeed will respond to that question with a YES. The majority will have reservations – and, of course it is here that you have your chance to introduce the idea of looking at the opportunity you are offering. It may only be as an immediate way of boosting their present income – but you could find you are talking to someone willing to consider an alternative occupation. If, on the other hand, the answer to the question is YES, the next question or two could run along the lines of 'do you think you pay too much tax?' This is a very emotive question indeed! – and almost everyone will answer YES.

'Is that because the job pays you too much money?' Again this is a question, without being in any way impertinent, that will open the floodgates! Once again, there is your opening to introduce the idea of extra earnings to augment those from the daily job.

A conversation of this sort, although quite light-hearted, must not appear at all flippant. This sort of approach *does* work – and is in no way devious. We are selling, not a product, but an opportunity – and, as with all selling, the first thing that must be established in the customer's mind is *a need*. In this case the need is for extra earnings or for a new opportunity – and, as with all sales situations, one must try to avoid the direct question. It is the direct question that will produce an automatic answer as part of a natural, conditioned defensive mechanism.

I hope you would now agree that it is no use simply confronting someone with an invitation to go to an opportunity meeting. They must, in their own mind, see the reason for such an invitation. Show most people a 'need' and you are very close to being able to convert that into a 'want'. Nobody buys anything *unless they want it!*

Don't become a nuisance to people – it is always a case of striking the right balance, of letting people know what you do, and getting them to realize that you could be of real help and value to them. Obviously not every situation will be fruitful. Do take care, though – nobody wants to become the sort of person whose reputation has preceded them, and others turn away from at a party!

Ask questions all the time and *listen to the answers*. If you wish to acquire the reputation of being an interesting person and a good conversationalist, *ask questions* and learn to become a good listener! If you are so fortunate that you are asked what *you* do, a very casual reply is all that is needed: 'I show people who need it how to add to their income – but let's not talk business at a party! Give me your phone number and I'll ring you in a day or two and explain what it's all about.' An approach like this works very easily. There are very few people who don't want to know how they could boost their earnings. Simply handing a person

48

your card and asking them for theirs is a perfectly easy approach. Its a strange fact of life, but people love handing out cards – and most people find it difficult to throw them away. Business cards, it seems have become collectable items, like stamps. Make sure, however, that your own card is of a standard size so that it will fit into a business card file because, once you're in there, you're in for keeps!

Everything you do and say must be aimed at creating trust and confidence. The need is to make people feel totally at ease with you, so avoid creating any unnecessary pressure – and this way, you will never be short of people to whom you can make that all-important presentation of the business plan.

The things we have been examining are all aspects of communication – and it must be your aim to become a master communicator. Eye contact is one of the most significant aspects of communication. Eyes are the window to every genuine emotion and will give you – and of course your prospect – all manner of reactive signals expressing empathy, acceptance and sincerity. Some cynic said, not without a degree of truth: 'sincerity! – easy! . . . anyone can be taught that!'

There was an incident recounted on the radio about the speaker's first meeting with a particular African. The man stared intently, deep into the Englishman's eyes and said simply, 'I see you'. The speaker said he experienced all the emotions of security and sincerity, not to mention a certain feeling of self-revelation, but the African's behaviour created an immediate bond of understanding between the two men.

One of the most effective methods of approach when seeking an appointment with people you don't know well is by telephone. When you initiate the call you are able to control the conversation and keep it to an absolute minimum. On the telephone one cannot be exposed so easily to being closely questioned. Avoid entering into a discussion of the plan and *never* offer morsels of it to your prospect in the belief that you are interesting them. Really, you are only giving them every opportunity to say NO because they do not have sufficient information on which to make a judgement – and NO represents the easy option. A well known American salesman used to say of telephoning for appointments, 'if I tell, I'm dead!' If you start explaining things and giving out *too much* information, all you are doing is diluting the professional presentation he would experience at an opportunity meeting. And because you *cannot* hope to make the presentation over the telephone you are again simply offering your prospect every chance to say they are not interested – even before they can possibly have taken in sufficient information about the opportunity to make a valid judgement.

Try smiling when telephoning – a smile can be 'heard' and can add a warmth and friendliness to the call. Don't be afraid to intrigue your prospect if you feel like it. 'This may, of course, not be for you at all – but something that might have a profound influence on your life has got to be worth taking a look at! Wouldn't you agree?' This sort of approach can be very disarming when you also point out that there is absolutely no obligation – and the idea you want to show them doesn't appeal to everyone, anyway.

The presentation to which you hope to invite people will have been put together with thought, reason and logic so as to guide the observer through a series of steps that lead towards a planned conclusion. Feeding snippets of the plan to a newcomer has about as much use as giving them one piece of a jig-saw puzzle and expecting them to understand the picture of which it is undoubtably a part.

It will sometimes be the case that an opportunity meeting is not scheduled for the very immediate future and you have people eager to know what you have to offer. This is one occasion when there is a good case for visiting them in their own home to make your own presentation of the plan. Perhaps, better still, in the early stages at least, get your sponsor to go with you to make the presentation.

However it is done, the all important thing is to get the appointments. Don't make the mistake of feeding too much information at any one time to your newcomer. Most people can only assimilate a certain amount of new material in any one session, and too large a dose can have the effect of diluting your message. So it is better to keep them hungry, waiting for more. Keep everything simple. Use ideas that are easy to duplicate – they will be remembered and have real value when your new recruit has to teach the next level in the developing network.

Never let a prospect think he or she is doing you a favour by agreeing to attend a presentation – on the contrary, it is *you* who are doing *them* a favour by exposing them to an opportunity that could completely change their lives. That should be worth the outlay of an hour or so out of anybody's evening, surely?

Statistically, only a proportion of those that attend a meeting will wish to take the matter further. Accept this as inevitable and never forget that those who don't take up the challenge should, if you are any good at the job yourself, become customers!

The great thing when you are at the beginning of a new adventure – and making your first approaches *is* an adventure – *is to START!* It is all too easy to procrastinate and put things off for one insignificant reason or another. Procrastination is death to creativity and is the graveyard of opportunity. It is always so much easier to do *nothing* than to do something!

So, just get on with it!

A tried and tested prescription for overcoming procrastination is to repeat 'do it now! – do it now!' 10 times morning and afternoon for 3 weeks – at the end of that time, according to people who have tried it, you will never procrastinate again!

There will be many occasions when your initial

approach to a prospect is face-to-face. All the same rules apply regarding exposure of any detail of the plan but you *must* be able to talk with a sense of urgency and excitement. Enthusiasm is very infectious and difficult to resist.

If you know anything about communication you will be aware that about 70% of human communication is visual. Everyone these days has heard something about 'body language' – the gestures, stances, postures that add so much by both affirmation and contradiction to what is simply being said.

We are hearing a message when someone is talking to us but, if we cannot *see* them, that is all we *are* doing – hearing the message. When we see as well as hear, the 'texture' of the message is enriched and embellished by what the eyes are saying, what the hands are doing. Body language has taken on a significance that almost makes it a science but, unfortunately, this is not really the place to explore it in any depth. Suffice it to say, yet again, that one should never attempt to sell the Network Marketing concept or a business opportunity over the telephone! It doesn't matter how good you think you are at explaining things – just remember this, if 70% of communication is visual, on the telephone *you are only 30% effective!* The telephone approach should only be used to secure an appointment so that you may meet face-to-face so that you can be 100% effective!

Body language is a great revealer of *attitude*. Posture expresses attitude just as attitude influences posture. Posture and attitude promote confidence and endow a person with both authority and credibility.

Getting people's interest is not at all difficult in a world in which most people are seeking some way to earn additional income to enable them to better their lifestyle, have more exciting holidays, get a new car, travel more – and generally have more disposable cash. We live in a climate in which almost *everyone* is our prospect, yet very few people have any idea how to obtain more of the good things of life, short of turning to crime!

There *are* those who find the idea of approaching others a little intimidating, even frightening. What then are the fears people have?

Fear that a prospect will not be interested. Networking is certainly not for everybody so there are bound to be people who cannot see the benefits you find exciting. Don't worry – these are all potential customers.

Fear of what others will think. Some people fear for their status – I doubt this would be a worry if they were perceived as very successful and earning a great deal of money!

Fear that they might be faced with questions they cannot answer. I used to tell young salesmen going out to see their first customer, *you* are the only person that knows it's your first interview! To the customer you are the expert and the professional. Even when you only have *some* answers, the customer doesn't have any! And there was one other thing I impressed on them. If you should be asked a question to which you do not know the answer, – *don't answer the question! Admit you do not know – but add that you will find out. That* is professional!

NOTE: see also the section on 'PROSPECTING' in Part II.

THE MOTIVATION

Motivation is the driving force in our lives. But a driving force can have little effect unless there is a defined destination and a plan to get us to it.

Before we attempt to do anything there must be a *desire* to do it or it is unlikely that we will ever make a start. The stronger the desire for achievement, the more likely it is to materialize. Real burning desire will prompt the thoughts and actions that will make a goal achievable. Total *belief* in our ability to carry out the plan by completing whatever tasks it may involve is almost as important as desire.

You may have designed the ultimate car and know without a shadow of doubt that it is capable of phenomenal performance. It is a triumph of design and elegance, brilliantly engineered, and it is standing on the gravel outside your front door. Everything about this splendid vehicle is right – it is the ultimate in every respect and yet it sits there in all its glory – unusable. It cannot move, it cannot fulfil its potential and is a totally useless object until *it has petrol put in the tank!*

Until that moment this inert, beautifully planned and conceived object could not function because there was nothing to motivate it – to move it forward and enable it to perform in the way that was intended.

In its simplest form motivation is what gets you

out of bed in the morning and sends you to work. This may be for one of several reasons:

1. The alarm clock has gone off and you know, automatically, that you are obliged to respond by sheer force of habit and obligation.

2. To enable you to live and to support those who depend on you, you must shift into gear, no matter how reluctantly, to go out into the world and do whatever life requires of you.

3. Because this is the start of a new day, promising unlimited potential, new adventures and experiences. Nobody knows just *what* will happen! The world is an exciting place!

The first two reasons for getting up represent what I would call *passive motivation* – a contradiction in terms – but a label that does describe the situation. Number three is real active self-motivation. This is an ingredient available to all, but to the self-employed it is *vital* and must be developed and nurtured constantly. It is what generates those flutters in the stomach, the quickening around the heart that promotes excitement – the glow of anticipation, the flush of foolish and unaccountable optimism! We are expecting a lot from life and, more particularly, of ourselves and are tuned to recognize and respond to any opportunity that offers itself on this exciting new day! That, then, is the nature of motivation. Now let's take a calmer look at the nuts and bolts of the phenomenon . . .

What is it that creates success? What makes us tick?

More especially, what is it that can make us tick faster or more effectively? It is what I have called the A-B-C of life.

ATTITUDE-BELIEF-COMMITMENT

Understand the value of these three things and you have, as near as anyone can come to it, the 'secret' recipe for success. But success at what? The Concise Oxford Dictionary – and here a dictionary definition has real relevance – gives one definition of success as 'favourable issue, accomplishment of end aimed at attainment of wealth or fame or position.' If you were to examine the attributes required to attain each of these three ends and amalgamate them, the result would be a general betterment in the attitudes and attributes of any individual – and this is what I suggest 'success' is all about.

Many people talk about success as being very much to do with 'winning'. I am never quite sure what this means since winning implies someone else has been beaten – and that person may be relatively successful, in his or her own right. This relative success could well be undermined through being eclipsed by the 'winner' – and in that context every other participant in the event becomes a loser.

In the quest for our own success, the last thing we should wish to do is dent someone else's ego. There should never be any need to take advantage of others – rather, we should be helping others towards their own goals and attainments. That way, in attaining *our* goals, we *grow* in stature and by so doing greatly enhance and enrich our own sense of self-esteem.

I would rather describe success as the achievement or attainment of goals – which in itself implies improved performance in some area of life – and not just the crushing of someone else! Real success, then, is improvement in all aspects of human behaviour. It is not, for example, sufficient to succeed in the attainment of great wealth for its own sake. That may have come about by the exploitation of less fortunate or less dynamic individuals, revealing a total lack of concern for the well-being of one's fellow men.

True success in any field, therefore, must be accompanied by a feeling of personal growth and the satisfaction of knowing that that in some way the actions which brought it about have benefited or improved a situation, helped an individual or brought some form of enrichment to life in general.

Success carries with it certain responsibilities. The responsibility to put something back either into life generally – or possibly into the situation through which the success or personal betterment was realized. There is a theory, that has a lot to commend it, which suggests that in the striving for and achievement of success, there is a 'tithe' to pay, a price, perhaps, to show gratitude and appreciation for the gifts your efforts have bestowed upon you. For example, to be prepared to set aside say 10% of one's earnings which, given to a charitable foundation, would help to improve the lives of less fortunate individuals than yourself, might fulfil such an obligation. This has always struck me as a very worthy concept – others might argue that it is too little or too much.

Great satisfaction too, comes through helping others to succeed. The principles of sponsoring and sharing that characterize Network Marketing, exemplify the whole notion of helping one another. The success of the individual is a shared experience through the involvement and supportive activity of others. Networking has the ability to bring people together in a spirit of mutual striving towards both individual and collective attainment. My experience has shown that the truly dedicated Networker is usually a genuine person who has discovered the right values in life.

Success or failure, good or evil, triumph or disaster – all lie within you. You carry the seeds of your own potential success – even your own destruction – with you at all times. Success or failure in life equates to how you handle the available ingredients. It has always fascinated me to see how, give the same ingredients for a recipe and the same set of instructions, half a dozen people can produce six different versions of the same dish. The implications for a parallel in life are quite fascinating!

If we accept this idea of unlimited potential – tempered, of course, with environment, upbringing and education – surely we must be prepared to accept responsibiity for our own lives and the directional deviations they have followed? It is too easy to blame all manner of outside agencies for our own short-comings. How often do we honestly face up to the fact that we are indeed responsible for ourselves and our actions?

It is not results that determine attitudes, *it is attitudes that determine results*.

Attitude is all about the way we perceive things, not least, the way we perceive ourselves. It is to do with the 'view' or standpoint we take in relation to other people and to almost every situation in which we involve ourselves. When attitudes are 'correct' our ability is at a peak of effectiveness and what follows as an outcome can only be worthwhile. Attitude is to do with 'doing things right' as well as 'doing right things'. The degree of enthusiasm we can bring to a task, will very much determine the success of its outcome.

'Body language' as just one aspect of communication has a great deal to do with attitude. It would not be inaccurate to say that speech is what we *say* whilst body language reveals what we actually *mean*. Attitude is expressed through posture and gesture – the visible aspects of communication – and, whilst we have reasonable control over our words, we have much less influence over our body language.

Enthusiasm is an attitude and is very much related to body language. It would be virtually impossible to experience real enthusiasm whilst moving slowly and making no bodily gestures. Mind and body are very closely linked in the expression of emotion. The drooping, bowed head and inward-turned gestures of grief, the raising of the voice, the flamboyance and exuberance of elation and the fast talking and urgent gestures of anxiety are all manifestations of the mind/body relationship.

Have you ever noticed how easy it is to convey attitudes to other people? We are all affected by genuine expressions of grief, elation, enthusiasm, excitement, appreciation and so on, but we are also unconsciously affected by a myriad of other mundane, pedestrian agencies.

A very simple example makes an amusing experiment. Next time you are standing talking to someone face to face, try folding your arms during the conversation. In no time at all the other person will mirror this gesture quite unconsciously – often followed by an observable realization of what they have done and an obvious attempt to undo the posture and alter it to a somewhat self-conscious display of nonchalant relaxation.

If you want someone to share your enthusiasm over an idea, try sitting forward on the edge of your seat as you face them. They will find it very hard not to do the same. The result – a sense of urgency and anticipation coupled with an attitude of heightened interest.

Attitude has a lot to do with self-image, with the way you like to or want to see yourself and the manner in which you care to present yourself to others. Do you respect yourself and see yourself as the equal of all men and women? Do you *like* yourself? Obviously in this business of Network Marketing it is essential that you have credibility, that people can easily *believe* in you. Credibility is entirely attributable to attitude. Not only must you positively exude confidence yourself but, in doing so, give others confidence. You must see yourself as successful to be successful. The value you place on yourself will be the measure others will willingly accept. Everyone likes to deal with obviously successful people so it is vital that in either appearance or actions you never under value the essential product – YOU! Dress the part, play the role and you will *be* the person you *feel* yourself to be.

Belief, our second vital attribute, has, as you can see, developed quite naturally out of attitude and everything we have said about it. But belief covers many aspects of our lives so we need to identify the forms it can take.

'I believe' has been said to be the most emotive phrase in the language – the two most powerful and meaningful words. So far as Networking is concerned, the aspects of belief with which we are concerned are:

1. Self-belief. The belief in your own ability to succeed. This must become a positive driving force in your daily life and must always be very much part of your awareness. Believing you are capable of doing something will point the way to *how* it can be done. Too often belief gets stifled by the worry about the 'how'. That is not part of the belief mechanism. Believe in *you* and *how* will take care of itself. The

person who always takes the line 'well I'll give it a whirl but I can't see how it's going to work' will never achieve a great deal simply because they are pre-empting failure from the outset – and not displaying the degree of belief necessary to carry the task through. It is only necessary to *suggest* to your sub-conscious that you don't entirely believe and it will present you with all the reasons to support that idea. That is where negativism begins.

2. Belief in the product or service you are selling or presenting. Your belief will give it credibility in the eyes of your potential customer. If you use it yourself and can genuinely enthuse about it you are endowing it with a veritable seal of approval. Your belief will sell the product more effectively than any advertising.

3. Belief in the concept of Network Marketing as a means of attaining eventual financial independence through the principles of sharing and sponsoring.

4. Belief in the particular company whose products or services you are representing.

Belief and sincerity go very much hand in hand and are both easily recognized when they are totally genuine.

Commitment springs very easily out of belief since it is the more practical side of realizing your dreams or desires. Commitment is the force that will provide the motivation to drive you forward to do all the things you know must be done to achieve true success. It is more directly related to action than either attitude or belief.

Never let the attitude of others effect you. Negatives tend to breed and are always on the look out for fertile ground as a place in which to germinate, so don't associate with negative people as they can so easily demotivate those around them.

Success comes from within YOU – don't let
the enemy in!

Having recognized the direction you intend to take – the goals – and planned the route you must follow to achieve your aims, then commitment is the extra ingredient that will provide the energy and drive to complete the journey. Without commitment it is doubtful that you would ever start!

Look to the future – that is where you will spend the rest of your life . . .

Attitude is the '*Here I am! This is me!*'

Belief is the '*I can do it!*'

Commitment is the '*Do it now! – and do it well!*'

and it all adds up to MOTIVATION

THE 100 DAYS
PLAN – AT LAST!

You will learn more by going out and doing the job than you will ever learn in a classroom situation. That is not to say training is not necessary – but nothing can take the place of hands-on-experience. It is the quickest way of ironing out the bumps, coming to grips with all the problems – and in a way that makes you think on your feet. Don't be afraid to make the mistakes that will, hopefully, never be made more than once!

Let's list the stages through which you will pass as you begin to develop your business:

STAGE ONE

1. Buy the product. Try the product. Develop belief in the product.
2. Be totally familiar with your starter pack.
3. Read all you can about Network/Multi-Level Marketing.
4. Attend all the meetings you can.
5. Learn to answer the key negatives – Pyramid Selling etc.

6. Learn the retail business.
7. Learn the presentation of your business and marketing plan.
8. Make a large prospect list – and keep adding to it.
9. Attend all the training meetings/courses available.
10. Qualify for any form of volume bonus as quickly as possible.

STAGE TWO

Once you have qualified for the all-important bonus that will enable you to start serious Network building, seek out and identify 5 people capable of doing exactly what you have done and make sure they have mastered all the items in STAGE ONE as soon as possible.

STAGE THREE

Help *your* 5 to find *their* 5. This will involve you in the one-to-one (1:1) interviews and with the training of 25 people. Whilst you are doing this you are preparing everyone for

STAGE FOUR

Still helping your 5 to train their 25 then helping that 25 to find their 125 . . . and so on . . .

IMPORTANT NOTE: As I pointed out in my introduction – but feel it is worth repeating here – this plan is based strongly on the idea of recruiting or sponsoring in *fives*. Not everyone preaches the five principle – some, for example recommend building in sixes and base their whole presentation on this. No matter! What we are dealing with here is a concept or theory developed with the idea of getting the beginner in Networking into a successful situation within a given time-frame – 100 days. Everything I am suggesting is just as valid whether you are building in twos, fives, sixes or whatever. The main principle involved is that your effort and energy is *contained* and channelled by the discipline of a system that keeps your recruitment within manageable bounds. One of the ingredients of success is to have the wit to recognize that flexibility of thinking is important! – be flexible enough to recognize that the 100 DAYS Plan is a *theory* not a rigidly laid down set of rules from which one must not deviate.

Your job is two-fold. You are marketing a product *and* offering a business opportunity. Don't try to separate these two elements in your mind as they are very closely entwined. Sales should come about as the natural outcome of building your organization. Most people don't like the idea of 'selling' and you must realize by now that you will never build a successful Network operation by putting total emphasis on selling.

Everyone you speak to is either a prospective customer or a possible recruit – and many will prove to be both. Don't, therefore, be too selective but approach people from either direction, depending on the feelings you get as your contact develops.

Obviously you will experience rejection. There is nothing *personal* in this – it is not *you* that is being rejected, it is the idea or concept. It is *not you* that will be the poorer for the rejection either. Always remember that there must be so many NOs before you get to a YES!

*IN BUILDING A SUCCESSFUL NETWORK ORGANISATION **THE FIRST 100 DAYS** IS THE TRULY SIGNIFICANT PERIOD.*

With this thought in mind, make a resolution not to be deflected from your purpose in any way. It is within this time frame that so many people have faltered, lost heart, and wandered away to try something else that might make their fortune for them. Believe this – *there are precious few other opportunities that can even **match** the potential you are investigating.* 100 days is no great commitment if the end result points clearly to the fact that you are on the way to very high earnings, financial independence and a life-style that goes hand-in-hand with those things. If you are going to see your life change significantly, three months is *nothing*! Anything worth having is surely worth striving for and worthy of a few sacrifices, particularly in the early days. The average family spends 35 hours a week watching television – if the only sacrifice you made was to give up television for say three evenings a week, and devoted that time to developing your new business, the results would repay you handsomely.

It is possible to make a map of success if you

accept that success is a journey, or a progressive state, rather than a destination. Let's make a 9 month map, the 9th month being our destination. A map, coupled with a time-scale is essential to any journey into unknown territory as it can, at any time, indicate just how far one has travelled, precisely where one is at any time, and how far one still has to travel.

Planning is going to be essential, and plans can often be made based on statistical facts. Knowing precisely what one must do to achieve a specific end can help a lot in allocating time to the various activities that will make up the daily routine.

A simple set of statistics can follow a pattern like this:

You invite 50 people to opportunity
meetings – 25 turn up
Out of that 25–20 show real interest
Out of that 20–10 actually attend 1:1
or 2:1 meetings
Out of that 10–5 come into the business

So what do these facts tell you? Simply that to bring one person into the business, you must find 10 that show sufficient interest to say that they will come to an opportunity meeting. That may mean you would have to contact say 15 to 20 initially – or, to get your initial five serious recruits, it would be necessary to make around 100 contacts.

Doesn't that bring home the importance of prospecting and always maintaining a good list of prospects? Doesn't it also demonstrate the importance of *really looking after your prospects* as they pass through the successive levels in the process of getting to that final commitment? If you are armed with statistics like these you are always on your toes because you *know* what the *likely* pattern will be. There is always the possibility that you can better the statistical averages by behaving in an above-average way! If you can then teach and motivate others to behave in the same manner, maintaining the standard of quality you have set, the development of your Network will be both swift and secure. *Go for the best* – anything less will dilute your development.

There is one other interesting fact hidden in those statistics – if you recruit 5 people out of a possible 50, there must have been 45 other opportunities to sell the product as well!

Your initial job then is to get five serious people in place and, at the same time, help and encourage them to each start to seek and identify their own serious five.

Now would it be reasonable to assume you could recruit one person per month and also sell 2 units of product per month? (I am assuming a 'unit of product' to have a value of around £100 to £150.) If you could do that, would it be reasonable to assume that each person recruited was capable of doing the same – recruiting one person per month and selling 2 units of product per month?

The real magic of Network Marketing is about to be revealed to you. . .

Month	Existing	New recruits	Total	Units of product
1	1	1	2	4
2	2	2	4	8
3	4	4	8	16
*100 DAYS				
4	8	8	16	32
5	16	16	32	64
6	32	32	64	128
7	64	64	128	256
8	128	128	256	512
9	256	256	512	1024

* Without knowing what product or products might be involved, it is difficult to know what one might expect monthly earnings to be at this stage, but a loose average figure that would fit the majority of companies would fall somewhere between £1000 and £2000 per month.

In month 9 your Network has built to 512 people and, between them 1024 units of product have been sold that month. Your earnings should look quite interesting! Not only that, but, by the very nature of Networking, you would have achieved a status in your organization that provided you with the extra monetary benefits that accompany different levels of production.

This simple plan is based on very modest and achievable goals. It demands only one thing – *THAT A CONSTANT LEVEL OF ACTIVITY IS MAIN-*

TAINED AND THAT YOU DON'T STOP UNTIL THE WHOLE PLAN IS ACHIEVED.

Do that, do it diligently, and you will succeed at everything you set out to achieve . . .

To summarize:

1. The key to any sucessful enterprise must be a good product.

2. The commitment to sponsor 1 new person per month and to sell 2 units of product per month.

3. To attend at least one training meeting per month.

4. Keep reading books and listening to tapes – and seeing your down-line do the same.

5. Maintain quality control. Maintain standards of integrity and ethical behaviour. Don't cut corners.

6. Keep checking that your presentation remains the same. Standardize everything. Don't try to re-invent the wheel.

7. Help your first and second levels to find and sponsor their five special people.

8. Always be on the look-out for Aces.

9. Keep in touch. Do not allow anyone to flounder.

10. Motivate by example. Lead from the front – beckoning not pointing. Real success comes from within you and from how good you are at communicating your message to others. MLM/Networking is about people not about selling.

PUTTING IT INTO ACTION!

What may look like a simple plan can so easily deceive the unwary by creating an atmosphere that is too relaxed. In that first 100 days you cannot afford to slacken the pressure. This is where the pace for the 9 months is set; 100 days represents a sensible point to take as a bench mark because by then a clear indication of realistic earnings will have materialized – thus providing the motivation to drive onwards for the remainder of the nine months – when your income might be so interesting that it really would represent a state of financial independence.

Work your plan from the hardest tasks to the easiest. Don't ever put off until tomorrow what you could do today. By planning your activity on a day by day, week by week and month by month basis you are almost certain to achieve your goals. It doesn't matter if you recruit too many people so long as you feel capable of *controlling* the situation. It is only if you don't achieve your monthly target that the whole plan begins to show the cracks. Most studies of human motivation have revealed that people are only happy when they are pursuing goals because doing that is, like recognition, very much fulfilling a human need. A goal is an achievement and a reward for activity. Without goals to achieve a human being is vulnerable to stress.

There are basically three different ways in which human beings will set about the attempt to improve their position by the achievement of goals. The first is by focusing complete attention on *where they want to be*. Their imagination is sufficiently vivid to persuade them that it is only a question of time and persistance, and they will get there. Their attempts are usually qualified by 'when' – when their ship comes home, when their luck changes, and so on.

The second type is the person who *knows where he wants to be* but never modifies his behaviour in his attempts to arrive. He will for ever go on doing the same old things, never *learning*.

The most sensible person sets himself goals and sub-goals, because that way, the journey becomes more interesting. Achievement of sub-goals along his way gives him great satisfaction and provides the necessary spur to keep him going until he eventually achieves his main goal.

The real key to understanding goal setting is to realize *where you are now*, not simply to fix your eye on where you are going. To use a golfing analogy, it is not *where the ball is going* that should be the focus of your attention, but rather *how you hit it*! If you hit it correctly, it has a very good chance of going where you would wish.

All of life is a comparison between potential (where we want to be) and performance (where we are now). The dream and the reality . . .

So goals are the very breath of life if we are to achieve anything of significance.

Many goals are too broadly based to be really effective. I am presenting this working plan to you the right way round. If I had said that the aim in your first 9 months was to sell 1024 units of product and be responsible for recruiting 512 people, you would have viewed the task as impossible. The psychology of goal setting is to start from the objectives (1024 and 512) and break them down, relating everything to a time-frame, until the goals become both reasonable and manageable (2 units of product and 1 recruit per month – *per person*).

To put your plan into effect as quickly as possible, make a start by going to every meeting you can. The content might appear a bit repetitious but the present-ation of the business and marketing plan will always vary from one person to another. You need to be exposed to as many variations as possible until you feel confident that you could undertake at least a part of such a meeting yourself.

Talk to people constantly. Never miss an oppor-tunity to tell anyone about the offer you can put before them – and make every effort to get people to go to the meetings with you. Don't tell them too much other-wise you are pre-empting the more professional explanation they will get at an opportunity meeting. It is possible also, that in your prospect's mind, you are inadvertently removing the reason for going.

It is perfectly possible to achieve the targets of the 100 DAYS plan on a part-time basis by being prepared to make the necessary time sacrifice, but let's examine the implications of entering the business full time and look at a few useful pointers to the changes this may make to your life-style.

To begin with, you will almost certainly be working from home. This is both practical and sensible as it alleviates any need for taking on expensive overheads. As things develop, you may build a team around you and make a collective decision eventually to take on office premises – and, of course, that way the costs would be spead.

Working from home requires discipline! You are working in your own natural comfort zone – the very place you do not associate with work! Some people find working at home impossible – others revel in it. Many need the habit and discipline of actually going to a place of work. Make a few rules for yourself. Start work at a specified time – just as though you were going to an office. You must impose disciplines of this sort since your hours will now be totally flexible. It is all too easy to drop into indolent habits when you have no supervision. Let your ambition be your supervisor! Never forget *why* you are doing what you have chosen to do. Once you get your Network well organized, your time will be much more your own and you can enjoy more flexible hours. *THAT FIRST 100 DAYS IS THE REAL CRUNCH TIME!* – and the time during which all the sacrifices have to be made. What you achieve over that initial period will be your stimulus to forge ahead for the remainder of the 9 months. If you have applied and committed yourself totally over the initial 100 days your working habits will have established a pattern – as well as earnings to justify all the effort – that will point to the real excitement still to come.

Use your time wisely and decide on your priorities. Your business will grow and expand in direct ratio to the amount of effort you expend on it, and people will respond to you according to the way you treat them – as you sow, so shall you reap! If you want a lot out of life, be prepared to put a lot into the process of living it!

Make sure you are never short of people to contact: keep your prospecting list topped up at all times. *Prospecting must become a habit.*

Aim also to develop a personal retail business as this way there is always the chance of new customers deciding to come into the business themselves.

Keep your recruiting under control until you have acquired sufficient expertise and experience to feel totally confident at handling the 1:1 meetings that will be involved. Remember, it is the responsibilty of anyone bringing others into the business, to teach them all they themselves have learned. If you recruit 5 good serious people, your wholesaler (sponsor) will almost certainly do the 1:1s for you. Your five people then go out and find five serious people for themselves – and you will be expected to handle a possible 25 1:1 meetings! Keep recruiting to fives – or whatever figure your particular organization favours. To achieve five really good people will almost certainly entail recruiting several more, but the extra people will very likely be those who only want to earn a bit of extra cash and be no more than retailers. This is all to your advantage as you will be supplying them with product and they will become a solid part of your own sales programme.

SETTING THE PACE

Being a pace-setter is no easy matter – but that is exactly what you are going to have to be. Your *attitude* towards your business and the people you hope to involve is all-important. You are setting an example and people will take their cue from you, and, to a certain extent, even imitate you since you are their sole means of example and motivation.

It can be very easy to motivate others on an immediate basis, just as it is easy to light a fire. But, as with the fire, unless the fuel supply is constantly renewed, the flames die down and the fire eventually fizzles out.

People who have been motivated too quickly can suffer from something not unlike withdrawal symtoms. Unless motivation is constant, depression can set in and destroy all the good work the motivator thought he had achieved. This is a situation often seen in large sales organizations who spend fortunes on their annual conferences to excite and motivate their sales force to new heights of enthusiasm and activity. One dose of this heady medicine really achieves very little, other than on a very immediate basis. If only there was a way to maintain some level of motivation throughout the year . . .

There is, of course! But it is far too simple to have much credibility with senior management who often imagine themselves to be too busy maintaining sales targets, recruiting more salesmen to promote growth and expansion, rather than paying attention to the simple human values that would raise the quality of the existing sales force by making more people effective and successful.

The most fundamental requirement for any human being is *recognition*. It is a far greater motivator than money – unless, of course, you don't have any! Everybody, regardless of what they do, will perform better, more effectively and with more enthusiasm if their efforts are constantly recognized. Recognition amongst peers is vital, not necessarily in the competitive sense, but in the sense of everyone being an important member of a team rather than just an individual always striving to *beat* his fellow man. Where the emphasis is on *winners* there must be, by implication *losers*.

Recognition is an on-going requirement. It is a fundamental mistake of management to assume that once an employee has demonstrated some degree of success in performance, and that success has been recognized – if only with a kind word or a pat on the back – there is no further need to continue the process. More good performers are lost through unthinking neglect than through any other single factor.

If recognition is withdrawn the person who has become used to it becomes depressed and performance begins to suffer. The employee feels neglected and imagines that he is no longer valued. As the decline progresses, his superiors begin to notice that he is no longer effective in the way he used to be, and thus begins a slow process of criticism, and perhaps even reprimand – it is all too easy to see how the general degeneration progresses.

So, in the planning of your developing Network, don't make the mistakes so often made in industry – remember the need for a constant level of motivation. Encouraging people to go to as many meetings as possible – regularly – will help to keep the fire fuelled. But your role must be to maintain contact with everyone you see as important and to pass on the need to develop the habit of contact and recognition right down the lines of Network expansion. Remember you are in a business of teaching and learning, learning and teaching, encouraging and fostering, recognizing and praising. People cannot thrive in isolation – and not providing sufficient recognition for effort can create a form of isolation. One word of warning – never ring anyone in your Network and ask how much they have *sold*. This would negate half the teaching and philosophy we have been spreading by placing particular emphasis on just one aspect of development. Ask them how they are progressing and what their successes have been – and then allow them to give you the answers. Try never to give the impression that there is any kind of competitive element in selling the product or you may be in danger of pushing that person down the wrong route.

In Networking, unless the level of enthusiasm is constantly maintained, it is very easy for people to drift away. This is why the 100 DAYS plan is so important. If the right degree of effort is maintained for that first 100 days, the beginnings of real success are virtually assured and the tangible results will be sufficient to keep your total interest alive. Within that 100 days there are bound to be times when the effort doesn't seem to be creating the desired result so it is essential that the level of support, motivation and recognition is maintained right up to the point where the sudden and exciting break-through occurs – and the real earnings materialize! But don't forget – the need for recognition is still there – even after that.

You now have, in your possession, a working model for achievement and success. Most of the people you bring into the business will be full of enthusiasm and interest. It is largely up to you how they develop from that point onwards. Some will inevitably become casualties of impatience – we are not involved in a get-rich-quick scheme – or suffer from insufficient interest to keep up the necessary level of activity. Many will learn all the lessons and begin to enthuse others as they start to teach all they have learned. This business is, above all, a teaching and learning process. This book is to help you to learn and to help you to teach others that they may do the same.

But, just to remind you again, there are some people who have an instinctive understanding of all the basic fundamentals we are discussing. These are the naturally successful people in life – those I referred to earlier as Aces. It is so important that you learn to recognize them.

The success of our Network depends on seeking out and identifying Aces because it is they who will immediately and instinctively understand the opportunity they are being offered – and exploit it without delay. They occupy the points in the pattern where quick and immediate growth takes place. They need all the encouragement and recognition you can give them as they will use their natural ambition to force the pace in their determination to demonstrate success. They will have a highly beneficial effect both above and below them in the line of development because of their example and infectious enthusiasm.

So, how do we recognize such people?

They are bristling with natural attributes, such as:

Always asking questions and requiring answers
Having a genuine interest in other people
Having boundless curiosity
Understanding the importance of goals and targets
Doing things *now* – not putting them off till later
Always having a very positive attitude
Being keen and anxious to learn
Having plenty of energy and natural drive
Being fun to be with

Whatever the Ace does, he or she will be successful at it because, above all, they have total *belief* in their ability to succeed.

The more Aces you can introduce into your developing Network, the faster it will grow and expand.

As we have said, anyone can *become* an Ace by sheer hard work and determination. Occasionally an Ace appears in a down-line development – a person who may have been there for some time. Quite suddenly, they spark off, and then there is no holding them back. Very satisfactory!

THE HABIT OF SUCCESS

Allow me to repeat a statement from some way back in the book: having recognized the direction you intend to take (goals), planned the route you must follow to achieve your aims, then commitment is the extra ingredient that will provide the energy and drive to complete the journey. Without commitment it is doubtful that you would ever start!

. . . and I would now add to that – **and without a plan it is doubtful that you would ever arrive!**

The 100 DAYS Plan is based on very simple statistics and could not, theoretically, be easier to follow. But, as I have already warned, a danger lurks within its apparent simplicity. In reality, a high degree of motivation is required to carry it through, and, to that end, some help to achieve the right mental attitude could be of benefit. Let's now aim to create a mental environment in which *expectation of*, rather than *hope for* success is the keynote.

It could be said that Network Marketing offers the chance of making people's dreams come true. The purpose of a 1:1 meeting is partly to uncover dreams and aspirations as these are the elements within a human being that can, handled correctly, become a strong motivational driving force. Mostly though, dreams are fantasies surrounding the things that our conscious mind regards as barely possible – little more than wishes and hopes – both rather nebulous attitudes which have little basis in reality.

But dreams – day dreams in particular –*are* important to us all. If then one can be instrumental in demonstrating that there is possibly a way to turn dreams into reality, something very significant would have been achieved.

To even begin to make these things possible, dreams and wishes must be replaced by desire, belief and expectation.

Anything the human mind can conceive and believe in is achievable

That is not an original statement but expresses an important fundamental fact.

We have talked a great deal already about belief as the all-important attitude when considering success and achievement.

The human mind, by the most simplistic of a layman's definitions, is divided into two parts. The conscious function is what we use ceaselessly as we live our daily lives and communicate both with others – through speech, sight, hearing, touch – and with ourselves – through thinking. The thought process is concerned far more with language than with visual images. Imagery does, of course, come into the process, but the pictures are accompanied by a constant 'voice over'. In the recognition function, think what is happening when, after tapping someone on the shoulder in the belief we know them, they turn, and we discover our mistake – it is only someone who bears merely a superficial resemblance to the person for whom we mistook them.

Our apology is instant! – but think of the miraculous process that has just taken place. Messages involving both words and pictures have been flashed to the subconscious 'computer' where they have been passed to the amazing memory bank of total past experience. They have been subjected to a process of sorting, evaluation and comparison to provide the feed-back that tells us we have made a mistake. *And the whole process took milli-seconds.*

The subconscious, like the computer, is programmable. Take, as a simple example, the act of walking. It is not necessary for us to 'think' how to walk. We would say this is because we 'know' how to achieve it. We did, however, have to *learn* the process through hard experience and constant practice – until all the information required to achieve this amazingly complex operation was safely stored, available for instant recall.

And so it is with every single movement we make. When we encounter a new task, new programming is taking place. If the task involves repetition, as with, say, a production line process, performance improves as familiarity with the task increases. Rehearsal and constant repetition produce better and more efficient performance as the flow of information and the resultant feed-back pass to and from the subconscious, constantly subjected to the process of adjustment, honing and polishing.

Why do we use the expression 'I'd like to sleep on it' when we are confronted by the need for the answer to a difficult problem?

Instinctively, it would seem, we are all aware that 'something happens' during the process of sleep which is vaguely to do with the solving of problems – *and yet so few people actually put this wonderful capacity to any real or intentional use.*

Your subconscious is capable of solving problems, not through a reasoning process, since its job is not to reason but to evaluate, and through that process provide indicators that will aid you in taking the correct action in relation to the original question. Don't be impatient. These answers are not necessarily going to appear immediately. But, be sure of one thing – they *will* appear. It is up to you to be alert and ready to receive the information which might come as a mere passing thought or a sudden hunch.

Your subconscious then, is a most remarkable piece of equipment, grossly under-used as a tool to aid us in achieving desired goals. Think of the resource you have at your disposal! Through deliberate pro-gramming, your subconscious can aid you in so many ways. Most of the things we do in our day to day lives are what we refer to as 'automatic'. But that is only like the walking process. Any automatic action has been learned, practised and perfected before the information is stored for constant use and the action becomes 'automatic' and can be achieved without 'thinking'.

Can you accept the idea, then, that success could become a habit?

Success is already within you. As the sculptor might look at a piece of stone and speculate on what lies within, waiting to be uncovered, it is possible for you to peel away the layers imposed by the years to uncover what is already there!

As with everything you have ever learned to do, it is possible to learn to be successful. The key to achieving this is simply your own total belief that it is possible. It then becomes a case of creating a set of programming instructions as the basis of what the subconscious is expected to do.

The very first requirement is that the instructions for the achievement of goals to be fed to your subconscious must be both credible and acceptable, but above all, *you must be able to totally believe in their accomplishment.*

All the instructions you use must be very straightforward and must be presented in the present tense, as though they had already been achieved – this is part of the 'believing' process that must go on in your conscious mind.

One very important fact to understand is that *it is not part of your role to consider **how** these goals are to be achieved.* That is the job of the subconscious – through its constant process of evaluation, to eventually present the feed-back that will provide the directional pointers that will show you what the next step should be.

It would be useless, for example, simply setting yourself a goal of 'a very large income'. This is so vague and loose that there is nothing to get hold of. So . . .

Lesson No. 1. *Define goals clearly and precisely*

'In my first 100 days I have achieved in income of £2000 per month.' That is a precisely stated goal – but, is it realistic? Can you really believe in its attainment?

If the truthful answer is NO, then re-state it in more attainable terms so that you *can* believe it.

Suppose you settle on an earnings target of £1200 per month as the figure. If you can accept this as achievable, you have set your first goal – 'In my first 100 days I have achieved an income of £1200 per month'. However, this contains no indication as to the way you expect to achieve this. It is just a sum of money sitting on your horizon with no visible route leading towards it.

Lesson No. 2. To provide your conscious mind with a plan, *break your primary goal down into sub-goals.*

A much-used example to demonstrate this is that of being confronted by the prospect of having to eat an elephant! The task, on first sight, would appear, not only bizarre, but totally impossible. Yet, if the beast was broken down into bite-size-pieces, given time it could be done.

You have a goal of £1200 per month. Through the 100 DAYS plan you already have the statistics that will dictate your activity:

Target: to recruit (sponsor) 1 new and enthusiastic person per month to sell a minimum of 2 units of product per month.

To achieve this: contact 20 people sufficiently interested to agree to attend an opportunity meeting.

approximately half will do this = 10
of this 10, 5 will get as far as a 1:1 Meeting,
of this 5, 1 PERSON WILL JOIN.

You have now established sub-goals – the bite-sized pieces – that relate achievement to a time scale. There are 22 working days in the average month. In your first 100 days then, you must contact approximately 80 people initially which equates to roughly 1 per working day. Obviously you are not going to be able to say every day that you have contacted one-person – things just do not work quite as conveniently as that. The whole point is that by establishing these milestones you have paced out the route and provided a measuring device to record progressive achievement within the context of your time frame. It is now always possible to know how far you have travelled and how far you still have to go – not forgetting, of course, how much time your have in which to do it.

Supposing in accepting the weekly target of 5 contacts as your yardstick, you also set yourself one absolute rule. When you over-achieve (say by an extra 5 contacts), you do not reduce the next week's target to zero! *You forget about the over-target-figure altogether.* However, and here comes the crunch, if you *under-achieve* (say by 2 contacts), *you ADD this number to next week's target!* So the following week you must contact at least 7 people. I am sure you can see the sense and reasoning behind this – you *must not allow yourself* ever to enter that 'comfort zone' which can so easily stifle motivation.

Lesson No. 3. *Don't cheat on yourself by making things too easy.*

Consistent achievement, though it might seem to be the aim of our planning, can have a stultifying effect on attainment and reduce it to something approaching mere boring routine. If achievement becomes too easy, look for ways to stretch yourself further.

Lesson No. 4. *The plan must always be flexible and adjustable.*

Re-assess your targets and start the clock again. The same degree of flexibility must be available when targets prove to be unattainable. Don't go battling blindly on, hoping that you can catch up. Regular under-achievement can have a very demotivational effect, so, as soon as the pattern is recognized, the immediate remedy will have to be applied – a bit of fine-tuning to re-establish a sensible target and the correct motivational values.

By now you will probably appreciate that if targets and goals are to serve the right purpose they must be set with care, thought and precision, but kept *just* out of reach to ensure that you are always that little bit stretched.

Lesson No. 5. *Once the 100 days are over, you have established a pattern*

The habit of success has been acquired! The real tasks now lie ahead – the continued building of your Network until you acquire that earning level that represents complete financial independence. This attainment – the completion of the 100 days target – now requires no more than maintaining the pattern you have set and entrenching yourself in **the habit of success!** Develop a sense of urgency! Remember – **successful people do what unsuccessful people don't do.**

Lesson No. 6. . . . *and what about the dreams?*

So far we have only dealt with the very practical things with which we wish our subconscious to assist.

Take a little time now to consider what you hope to achieve by entering Network Marketing – really to *think* about the changes it could bring to your lifestyle?

Think about all the things you have dreamed of in

the past. Are they still the things you would like to see happen, or the things you would dearly like to acquire? Why not write down everything you would like to achieve and acquire – and do it right now.

Again, do this in the present tense and with a certain amount of detail:

'I am totally financially independent'
'I do not have any debts'
'I own a house . . .' *and describe its location accurately.*
'I own a new car . . .' *again describe it accurately – make, colour etc.*
'I have at least two holidays a year – and go anywhere I wish.'
'I am able to eat out whenever I choose.'
'I have as much time as I want to be with my family'
. . . and so on . . .

It is quite a good idea, once you have established your list and refined it to transfer each individual item onto individual postcards. Each night, just before going to bed, and again first thing each morning, take out the cards, stand before a mirror and read what is on each card *out loud* several times over. If you feel unable to read out loud, at least whisper, but loud enough that you may hear yourself. You will be surprised how relaxed and yet curiously exhilarated you will feel doing this!

What is actually happening through this process is that you are impressing your requirements on your subconscious mind – and it is *that* which is actually going to help bring about the realization of the things you *desire*. As I have said – and it is important to remember this – it is not for you to question *how* these things are to be realized, but simply to *believe* that they *will* be.

All that is required is to get on with your life, doing the things you know you have to do and following the dictates of your inner voice.

Listen to its messages and *act* – without hesitation.

Some people might call this 'inspiration', others may use the word 'intuition' – or simply 'having an idea right out of the blue'. By now, I think, you must have a pretty good idea where these things, whatever name we give them, actually emanate from!

SECTION TWO
NUTS AND BOLTS

THEME AND VARIATIONS

In some of its forms Network marketing becomes very like a gigantic profit sharing scheme in which the consumer is also the commission earning distributor, a system where no real 'selling' takes place all.

Schemes of this sort have become known as 'matrix' schemes. The participant merely undertakes to purchase an agreed value or volume of product on a regular monthly basis. This may be for his own consumption although he can, should he wish, sell on to friends and neighbours. The so-called self-stacking matrix is a relatively new development in Network and Multi-Level Marketing. Each plan or system is described by a formula – for example 2×10, 2×12 etc. – indicating the pattern through which the plan builds.

These schemes offer the potential for extra earnings without too much effort since many do not involve meetings and can comfortably be developed from home, some totally by post and telephone. This, I suspect, is also their limitation to the truly ambitious person; they certainly have an attraction for the participant with no real ambition or highly developed sense of commitment. Another aspect of such pro-grammes is that, not having a need for constant association with other people, there is always a danger of demotivation through isolation.

I don't wish to give the impression that I am over criticizing matrix schemes. There are people who run highly profitable personal businesses on the 'portfolio' basis but it requires a special sort of organizational self-discipline to handle this particular situation well. The danger is always that it is too easy to dissipate one's energies over so many different programmes that none is handled really effectively. Look at it this way: if an individual can give 100% of his effort to one project, the likelihood of success is considerable. If his energies are divided between two projects he has reduced his chances by 50% in each case, if he is involved in four, the reduction is 25%, and so on. And, of course, if the programmes require regular monthly outlay, a lot of cash is going out. To truly prosper constant growth must be taking place. There are those people I mentioned in my introduction who will join everything – they are the MLM junkies – but rarely succeed to any great extent because they do not understand what is required to handle a portfolio successfully.

If I was to give one piece of advice to any newcomer to Network or Multi-Level Marketing, it would be this:

Choose one conventional MLM or Network scheme whose product you can really believe in and be prepared to follow the 100 DAYS plan to the letter, not deviating or letting up in any way. By doing this you will become aware of exactly what Network Marketing is all about and what it requires

from the individual. You will acquire the habit of hard work and *the habit of success* and see the rewards that can result from a high level of activity. As someone once said: – success begins when the habit of hard work is acquired.

At the end of the 100 DAYS you will have proved to yourself that either you are, without any doubt, doing the right thing, or that you are not really cut out for Networking in its true form. That is the point at which you might look at the matrix schemes and the idea of developing a portfolio. The point I am really trying to make is that, if you are looking at Networking as a means of earning a lot of money, give yourself every opportunity for it to happen!

The people who have done well with the portfolio idea – and there are some notable examples – will often point out the parallel of stock market investment. Spreading one's financial resources over a wide variety of investment situations obviously minimizes the risk of loss. But to the adventurous person who is still probably in an employed situation, *there is nothing to lose by really going for it!* In golf the most interesting player is the person prepared to take a risk – to play a shot that has an element of danger in it which, if it comes off, gives the greatest satisfaction and a real thrill of achievement. The alternative is always to play the safe shot and be a dull but good player. There is nothing wrong with that – these things are all a question of temperament and attitude.

The production (or sales) in matrix operations is

'automatic' through regular monthly commitments. This obviates the need for making sales and leaves the operative freer to concentrate on the development of his network. Even the 'recruiting' aspect is simplified. In the examples I quoted at the beginning of this chapter, the 2 represents the number of people one can sponser in the 'front line'. The 10 or 12 refers to the number of levels on which commissions will be paid.

The fundamental difference between the mechanics of matrix systems and the more conventional or 'pure' MLM or Network concept is that, in a matrix, it is not possible to sponsor in width – everything is geared to depth. If an individual sponsors more than two people, the residual recruits are placed in the matrix in the first available positions further down in the pattern – hence the expression self-stacking is used to describe this system. Each operative has a front line of 2. Their second level, is 4 (2 people sponsored by each of the front-line 2) and so one, doubling up at each level.

At level 10, following this principle through, there will be a total of 2047 people in a matrix, including yourself. All these people have a monthly commitment to buy a specified amount or value of whatever product is involved, so commissions – theoretically – can be considerable.

I hold a certain scepticism with regard to matrix systems because too many of them involve products of doubtful quality and value – the emphasis, in a lot of the publicity material I see, concentrates on the matrix development and the startling theoretical earnings, rather than on the product, which, too often, appears to be merely incidental. Far too many people join in matrix schemes in the expectation that everything is going to happen automatically and the earnings will begin to appear as the result of some mystical process that doesn't involve them in any great effort. They will be sadly disillusioned. Retention is another problem, and the fall-off rate is considerable. It all comes back to people working in isolation. The self-discipline required is considerable and this is not a situation with which everyone can adequately cope. Many matrices suffer from what we might call the Gruyere Cheese Complex – they become full of holes! I wonder whether, since these 'self-stacking' schemes are not really *pure* MLM, they should be known by a new name – perhaps MATRIX MARKETING?

The High Street of every town and city in the country is a showcase of examples of successful businesses that have become household names, and such developments have come about through a process remarkably like Multi-Level or Network Marketing – developing in a network pattern as branch succeeds branch. The operation we are concerned with is remarkably similar, simply substituting people for the shops.

When a manufacturer or provider of a service decides that Multi-Level or Network Marketing is the route he wishes to take, what are the first moves he makes?

Firstly he must find and appoint enthusiastic people in the areas of his operation to fulfil the role of key distributors. Once these founder members have been located and identified, it is their job to set about the task of spreading the word and building the down-line organization through which the product will begin to flow. Clearly, being key people, the initial distributors must totally believe in the product and the integrity of the manufacturer, indeed, become its disciples, since it is they whose role it will be to motivate others. Their enthusiasm must be of the highest degree as this is a most infectious attribute, easily transferable to others given the right conditions and environment in which to flourish. Their motivation would normally be no great problem since, in this all-important key role, their earnings are likely to be very high indeed. The success of the company depends on them, just as their success and earning potential is very much dependant on the stability of the comany.

Like a developing culture the cells begin to divide and multiply as the network starts to grow and successive levels of down-line development take place. I have described the development of a MLM organization elsewhere* as relying on a very simple basic principle – the concept on which all of life is based – a family tree, the creation of one generation from another. Through this process certain generic information is passed through the reproductive process from one generation to the next, information that is essential to the family's successful survival and continuance. Networking/MLM works in just the same way –

* 'Network & Multi-Level Marketing' by Allen Carmichael, Concept.

through a process of teaching successive levels as they develop one from the other to form the generic chain that is our network.

Some companies engaging in Networking put a very definite emphasis on selling. Hardly surprising – since the aim of any manufacturer *is* to sell his product. Selling though, as we have seen, is only one aspect of what Networking is all about. Networking is a method of marketing, and marketing is the concept from which selling is the end result.

Another approach places its main emphasis very much on recruiting. The primary activity is to seek out people to whom you wish to offer the business opportunity that has so excited you. Where, you may ask, do the sales take place, for without products moving nobody can possibly be paid or earn anything? The committed Networker buys and uses the product himself thus demonstrating his belief in it and providing the necessary credibility platform from which to impress and interest others as he builds his business. He 'shares' the product with others through his enthusiasm and belief, thus demonstrating that the purest sale that can be made is that in which your customer *asks to buy from you!*

The *ideal* situation is a combination of the two concepts, but with the added proviso, that the products being marketed are either consumer goods or products that will have to be replaced or renewed at some time in the future. This way on-going sales are ensured.

If your product range can be seen to have obvious

advantages, whether that be through price, originality, or quality when compared with its competitors, and if your obvious belief and enthusiasm cause it to sell – or better still, *be bought* – the likelihood of you finding people to sponsor will be very high indeed. You are playing both ends against the middle to the very best advantage – neither selling nor recruiting in the accepted sense, but simply sharing and sponsoring as a natural outcome of your own excitement. And, to add one extra benefit, if the product is consumable or repeatable, you will never be short of business as your customers will always be there to come back for more!

THE MEETINGS

As your interest in Network Marketing develops you will be more and more exposed to various types of meeting that are part of the pattern of building a successful business. It is important that we explore these in a bit more detail because part of the management of your own business will involve you in organizing and actually running meetings of each sort. The meetings should be designed to be both interesting and informative, providing a good data base covering all the basic information any newly sponsored candidate should need. There are three basic types of meeting used within most organizations, and each has its own very particular character and purpose.

1. The Opportunity Meeting
2. The One-to-One or the Two-to-One Meeting
3. The Training Meeting

Before we examine each in turn, let's lay down a few general guide lines. Credibility and professionalism should be the keynote of any meeting. The important factors are . . .

Being seen to be successful.
Representing a company with a fine track record and impeccable credentials.

Marketing some great products.
Presenting the products, the business opportunity and
the marketing plan in a thoroughly professional
manner.

1. THE OPPORTUNITY MEETING

The fundamental purpose of this meeting is *introduction*. To introduce the company, to introduce the products and to introduce the concept of Network Marketing.

Meetings must start promptly at the advertised time. They should be held in a 'neutral' venue – the conference facilities of smaller hotels are ideal if the numbers warrant it. This is all part of building both image and credibility. If we are offering business people a great business opportunity, let's make sure the venue is business-like too.

Some organizations suggest that opportunity meetings should be held in domestic surroundings. This may work occasionally but, generally speaking, the domestic venue is far too cosy and not at all suggestive of any serious business intent. The surroundings can be distracting and all the trappings of the homely domestic scene can so easily undermine the credibility of the opportunity being presented.

There should be a structured format to opportunity meetings that can be accepted as a template by everyone who is to participate in the development of the Network so that, wherever meetings are held, the pattern is always the same.

1. *An introduction to the company* – the manufacturer of the product, or provider of the service. This should include a brief history of the company, its founders and its original aims. Facts and figures help to give substance to the message and should be included to illustrate company growth and development over the years of its existence. Any other useful information to enhance credibility, such as Dunn & Bradstreet ratings will add greatly to the picture being painted.

2. *The product or service.* The product range should be discussed, bringing in anything that testifies to uniqueness in comparison with any competition it may have. Anything that enhances the image of the product should be included, particularly any independent assessments of performance, consumer testing reports and, in fact, any information that demonstrates both quality and value.

3. *The opportunity.* This will take the form of coupling the company image and the product with the marketing plan which ought to include a brief explanation of how Network Marketing operates. An uncomplicated description of how the commission structure works will also be useful, coupled to a time-frame – or some indication of the length of time it might take the average new entrant to see the expected benefits.

An opportunity meeting should end with a summary of the crucial points:

1. A stable company, with both strength and financial viability.

2. A company with an excellent history and track record.
3. Products of high quality and easy marketability.
4. A warm marketplace.
5. Products that are priced to sell.
6. Products that provide a good profit margin.
7. Products that are consumable or renewable.

After running possibly dozens of opportunity meetings it can be a temptation to deviate from or vary the content – indeed it can sometimes be difficult to remember what the aims of such a meeting are. This is why it is so important to have a pattern or template – so the original intentions never get lost.

The audience will be made up of people who are there because they are intrigued about an opportunity that might have the effect of altering their lives – they have not come to see a personal performance, no matter how dynamic – so ego trips are out – as is prima donna behaviour! The speakers are likely to be highly motivated people – very necessary to an occasion that should convey a sense of anticipation and excitement to the audience. It goes without saying that all speakers should be smartly dressed – if you are badly dressed, people remember your clothes: if you are well-dressed, they remember *you*!

The whole event should be staged with precision and professionalism, keeping to a strict timetable. If all these points are taken into account the maximum benefits will accrue to everyone.

An opportunity meeting also offers people already in the business a chance to get together. Most first-timers will be there as the guest of someone already involved, and it should be the intention of everyone to generate an atmosphere of friendliness and fun, giving the whole event a bit of a 'sizzle'.

Such meetings are useful as a boost to *everyone*. It is encouraging to those still learning and intriguing for those merely looking. Many people spend a lot of their time working in isolation, so the opportunity meeting, as a get-together, preserves a sense of reality and emphasizes the importance of each individual feeling a part of something.

Everyone should always gain some useful crumb from every meeting – the learning process never stops. Either you need the meeting, or the meeting needs you.

Before the meeting:

1. Tell your guests the format the meeting will follow – not the content, *just the format*.

2. Make sure your guests know the starting time, the venue, and how long the presentation will last.

3. Tell them what to do on arrival, where to go, how many will be there etc.

Best of all – personally take your guests along, especially if the meeting is to be a big one. Remember, people new to the business do not know anyone and can feel both vulnerable and self-conscious if left on their own. They could even drift away if you, the only person they know, don't show up. So, if you really cannot meet them beforehand – DON'T BE LATE!

During the meeting:

1. Don't keep dashing off to talk to people you know. Sit with your guests. Show an interest in them. Make sure you introduce them to as many people as possible. Give them a sense of belonging and involvement right from the outset.

2. Don't let misunderstandings remain unexplained, or objections remain unanswered.

3. Don't hesitate to fill in any details that the speakers may have missed. Supply as much information as possible.

After the meeting:

1. Bring anyone you know to meet your guests, especially if you can produce someone who is very successful or very experienced.

2. Answer questions as fully as possible.

3. Provide your guests with any material you can to maintain their interest. It is essential to keep this alive, so lend your guest anything that might be of help – and, within a day or two at the most, make arrangements for the second type of meeting –

2. THE ONE-TO-ONE (1:1)

This, as the name implies, is a much more informal and personal affair and yet it is possibly the most important meeting of all because it should be designed to promote decision and commitment on the part of the candidate. The underlying and ultimate objective of the 1:1 meeting is *to obtain a definite commitment*.

The meeting, ideally, should be conducted in a 'serious' environment such as an office or interview room. The real purpose is to explore the candidate's feelings, identify his or her dreams, aspirations and ambitions, to answer all the questions that will inevitably surface, and to dispel any doubts by providing sensible answers to all possible objections.

Remember to keep the meeting as informal as possible so start by relaxing the candidate with a little general chat. Ask why they are there. Is it because they have been made redundant or simply because they want to earn a bit of extra cash? Or do they want to develop a new career? Remember that old adage . . . you have two ears and one mouth – use them in that proportion. Ask questions and question answers – and, above all, *listen*.

Have you tried the product?
What do you think of the company?
Have you come across Network Marketing before?
Are you convinced that this opportunity is for you?
Do you understand the commission structure?
Do you understand the basic concept of Network Marketing?
What do you want for your future?
Why do you want those things?
When do you want them by?

These are just a few questions – the answers will lead you into all the explanations you must give. The final three are designed to bring attention back to the commitment. Keep control of the conversation, answer all the questions and the candidate's commitment should follow quite naturally.

One most important aspect of these personal meetings is to discover the aspirations and ambitions of the candidate – to probe until you discover his or her 'hot button', the thing that turns that person on. Once the candidate can identify the opportunity you are offering as the means of achieving the goals and realizing the dreams that he has revealed to you, he is well on the way to making the necessary commitment.

Motivation is an odd process. It is no use trying to motivate a person by telling him of the things that motivate you. Every one of us has secret ambitions – often merely pipe-dreams, hopes and wishes that we don't really believe will materialize. The things that represent one person's hot button may be completely meaningless to another.

If the situation still doesn't 'close' itself easily, the fault most likely lies with you. Ask the simple question: 'is there anything you feel I haven't explained clearly?' Reluctance to make a commitment often centres on some small point that the candidate hasn't fully understood – a point you may not have developed to his complete satisfaction – and don't expect everyone to tell you this!

It might be some time before you, if you are relatively new yourself, feel able to conduct a good 1:1.

This is where the Two-to-One (2:1) comes in. The very title of 2:1 perhaps suggests an unfair balance. The idea of the 2:1 is definitely not to overwhelm the interviewee by out-numbering him! The 2:1 interview is conducted by your sponsor whilst you, as you are also still learning, sit in on the interview and contribute in any way you can, ideally at the invitation of your sponsor when the time is appropriate. Two people can give the content of the interview different perspectives. The newcomer may recognize you as a kindred spirit – a relative newcomer like himself – and, to some extent, will tend to psychologically align himself with you and ask questions about your own experience. Your sponsor will, if he is good at his job, give you greater credibility in the eyes of your recruit by amplifying and confirming much of what you have already told him or her in other conversations. In its professionalism – and that is how it should appear – the 2:1 interview can provide you with 'the seal of approval' in the eyes of your new recruit.

If they have been successfully conducted, both a 1:1 and a 2:1 should end in a relaxed atmosphere with the commitment of the candidate and his/her willingness to sign a registration form and pay any necessary entry fee.

3. THE TRAINING MEETING

These are obviously an on-going feature of natural development. Some companies run very professional training courses which may last as long as a week. There may be a charge for the course. Don't forget – *you are self-employed!* A good training course will always represent money well spent and should be regarded as part of your investment in *you* – and remember, it is a tax-deductable item.

Later in the cycle of events there will be motivational seminars, meetings at which achievement is publicly recognized, and, depending on the particular organization, occasional large national conventions, rallies, seminars or even overseas conventions to which whole families may be invited.

If all this is beginning to sound a bit obsessive you must realize that, even when the-opportunity-of-a lifetime is on offer, people need constant motivation to keep doing all the things that will provide them with the benefits the opportunity has promised them. In reading this book, *you* should have a pretty good idea already as to why maintaining motivation is so important. If it is possible to have laid the corner stones of financial independence in 100 days, your activity pattern will be so well established that to continue working in the same way will be no problem!

OBJECTIONS – ELIMINATE THE NEGATIVE

Questions do not represent a *threat*! Treat them always as a genuine expression of interest, since that is most likely what they are. That way they will always be easy to answer.

Let's look at some of the most common points that will arise either as innocent questions, serious worries or downright objections:

1. IT'S PYRAMID SELLING ISN'T IT?

There are times when the best way to counter a question is by questioning the question itself – it often has the effect of causing the questioner to reveal his/her own lack of knowledge thus giving you the opportunity to provide the real facts.

So, ask what the questioner *means* by Pyramid Selling. You will very quickly realize that he has only the vaguest idea himself. There is no such thing as 'Pyramid Selling' nowadays.

'Pyramid Selling' has found its way into the Oxford English Dictionary which describes it as 'a form of financial trickery . . .' – and that, as a definition expresses no doubts! It was the name given to the now illegal schemes which were rife in the 1970's

119

and required participants to pay hefty entry fees as well as to commit themselves to sizeable purchases of stock, tempted into these extravagant orders by larger and larger discounts, the greater the volume purchase. At the time the press was full of stories of distressed people with mountains of products for which they had no immediate buyers. We, the public, have very long memories and the image of Pyramid Selling does indeed die hard. Most people who claim never to have heard of Network or Multi-Level Marketing will have heard of Pyramid Selling.

Network and Multi-Level Marketing are strictly controlled by the legislation that outlawed Pyramid Selling. Schemes are watched over by the D.S.A. (Direct Selling Association).

Network Marketing should be, and generally is, concerned with the marketing and distribution of products of both value and quality. The price to the consumer, at whatever level the sale takes place, must never vary and the commission system should be designed to benefit the largest number of people without taking advantage of anyone.

2. IS IT LIKE A CHAIN LETTER?

It is nothing like a chain letter. There are literally millions of people involved in Multi-Level or Network Marketing throughout the world. A great many of them, involved full-time, are making a very adequate regular income by having devoted themselves to the planned and structured building of a business using the principles of MLM. Whoever made a living through chain letters? There are those who will tell you they have, but *have you ever met one face to face?* I haven't! I've met a lot of people who have sent money off through chain letter schemes and received *nothing* in return . . . Legislation now governs chain letters so the instigators of these schemes – and I use that word deliberately – now hide behind the notional idea of paying money to be put on a mailing list or paying money to buy 'reports' that have little value other than as vehicles to apparently legitimize what would otherwise be illegal. The only people chain letters regularly benefit are photo-copying shops and list brokers to whom one is referred by most chain letters, as the means of acquiring the necessary number of names and addresses. At the time of writing. I get at least two chain letters on average every week in my post – and they come from all over the world! If I was to respond to each one of these unsolicited invasions of privacy in the manner laid down in their instructions, I would be outlaying something in the region of £1500 per month in photocopying, postage, and the purchase of mailing lists and envelopes! I make no apology for going on at such length about chain letters because if I can be instrumental in stopping anybody from wasting money in supporting these foolish ideas, I shall feel something has been achieved.

3. I KNOW SOMEONE WHO WENT INTO SOMETHING LIKE THIS AND FAILED.
So what?! We all know of people who have 'failed' at all manner of things. A car salesman can fail at selling

cars. That doesn't mean car selling ceases or suddenly becomes a worthless occupation. It simply means that cars go on being sold by the people who are best suited to sell them.

Network Marketing does, without doubt, attract many people who are looking for an easy ride. The get-rich-quick attitude sees Networking as a suitable vehicle. It *is* possible to make a lot of money in this business, but only by serious and sustained effort – but the true get-rich-quick exponent doesn't rate hard work very highly. The result is usually that he stays poor indefinitely whilst his search continues.

The person who fails in MLM or Network Marketing does so usually for one of two basic reasons. Either it is through laziness, possibly under the delusion, as we have just seen, that there are rich pickings to be had for little or no effort. The other is that his sponsor hasn't explained the concept well enough, and/ or given the newcomer sufficient help and support.

Everyone coming into MLM and encountering it for the very first time is naturally sceptical, a little uneasy and suffering feelings of insecurity. Support in the early stages is of vital importance and must be the main function and role of the sponsor. It is his job to keep in constant touch with those he is sponsoring until he is certain that they are totally confident in what they are doing. They represent, after all, a very important vested interest.

4. I COULD NEVER SELL ON THE DOORSTEP.
Most people, it seems, have the idea that they *know*

what selling is all about! They will tell you door-knocking is not for them! If this is what anybody thinks they are looking at, they have totally misunderstood *everything*! The whole philosophy of 'sharing' absolutely negates any idea of door-to-door selling. The distribution of goods and services – sharing – comes about as the natural outcome of meeting people and building relationships. Once your customers have experienced the products and like what they have found, they will come back for more and so an on-going situation develops which will keep your business flowing.

Nobody will be surprised if you don't like the idea of selling – statistically only 3% of the population do! The relationship we develop is just as important as the product. People buy from people and it is your credibility, integrity, charm – or any other positive characteristic – that is the vital ingredient in the sales formula. The simple answer, of course, is that in 'sharing' we are generally dealing with people we know who want and need a product we can provide.

5. I CAN'T AFFORD TO START MY OWN BUSINESS

This is not a terribly significant objection since the cost is minimal if your prospect starts by degrees – part-time at first whilst he or she maintains their employment. It is only at the point when they can clearly see they could at least match their present income, that they should consider going into MLM full time.

Starting in most MLM situations doesn't usually

require any great outlay other than time and effort –
and one cannot put a price on that.

6. MY WIFE/HUSBAND ISN'T INTERESTED, OR, DOESN'T WANT ME TO GO INTO IT

This objection is often the result of a husband or wife
going to an opportunity meeting on their own, being
taken through the presentation of a business and
marketing plan professionally, by a person skilled in
the presentation, then going home, full of excitement,
expecting to instantly convey what they feel to their
spouse! Frankly it is expecting a lot of anyone! The
inevitable outcome is disappointment and frustration;
it is hardly surprising that the enthusiasm is not
shared! The danger in this situation is that hurt
feelings can turn into resentment – and the exciting
new venture gets off on the wrong foot right from the
start.

Whenever possible, do make sure that you speak,
right at the outset to *both* parties and, if possible, get
them *both* to attend the opportunity meeting – even
though it may only be the intention of one of them to
join. Understanding and support are of great value and
importance between spouses. Their shared interest
and excitement will ensure things develop in the right
way, through their mutual vested interest and involvement.

7. I DON'T HAVE THE TIME

Pure procrastination! This should really read – *I don't
want to make the effort*. It can also be tantamount to

saying 'I'm not interested'. The only people who don't have time are those with their names in the newspaper obituary columns. Everyone has the time to do the things they *want* to do. If a genuine opportunity presents itself and you really want to do something about it, *you will*! It's not so much not having time, as rearranging one's priorities. Balancing one's time is often just a question of making a small sacrifice – like watching a bit less television! Surely if a new occupation has the potential to alter your entire life-style and open up new areas of possibiity in every direction it is worth a small sacrifice? If your prospect persists with the 'I don't have the time' objection, he or she is clearly not a person who would succeed – simply because there is no real *desire*. All success starts from that point. No journey can ever be made, no matter how long, unless the first step is taken.

8. I'M TOO BUSY . . .
This objection lays itself wide open to being turned around very quickly – to the surprise of the objector! 'Spendid! I always have the greatest admiration for people who use their time effectively. They are people who get on with things and are always open to new ideas.' Anyway, try it and see what happens!

9. WHO BUYS THE PRODUCT?
If the product was not constantly on the move, nobody could possibly earn any money. All the members of a Network will, because they believe in the product, be users or consumers of it. Sales occur constantly at all

levels in the organization – example is a great motivator. As the Network expands, so the volume of sales must increase. The ideal product for Networking is one that is either consumable or renewable, ensuring continuity of sales far into the future.

10. DO I GET A PROTECTED TERRITORY?
If you did, it would not be long before you felt very restricted! The very nature of Networking is that you can recruit people into your organization *anywhere* – even, in some schemes, world-wide. You recruit people where you find them – it is always possible to make arrangements to take care of the practical details of recruitment on a localized basis. Territory protection is *territorial restriction*.

11. I READ IN THE PAPER . . .
Newspapers will always pick up anything the least bit unsavoury and enlarge it almost out of recognition. In any industry there will be a few who try to exploit situations and/or their fellow men to their own advantage. In Networking there have been examples of exaggerated claims for products, getting people to meetings by the use of dubious and misleading information. Misleading information being disseminated at meetings, and the publication of product or recruitment advertising of a doubtful nature. Fortunately companies and organizations, for the sake of their own reputations, are swift to jump on any reported malpractice and, generally, control is very good.

12. WHAT HAPPENS WHEN YOU SATURATE THE MARKET?

Based on the fact that this has never yet been known to happen with any product, there is a strong case against saturation. There would never be sufficient networking operatives to cause saturation by either new recruits or products. The company that has been in the Networking business longest – over 20 years in Britain – still has less than .01% of the population of this country acting as its distributors. Far more people are born in any given period than enter Networking schemes in the same period. No matter how many new sponsorships occur, the largest organizations have their annual 'cull' through the system of re-registration, so the numbers of really serious and successful operatives grows slowly.

13. YOU HAVE TO BE IN AT THE BEGINNING TO MAKE THE REAL MONEY

Quite true! And of course, *you are*! You are always at the apex of the Network organization that starts with you. Networking probably represents the nearest thing to *true equal opportunity* in the entire business world. Anyone can build an organization just as large as they like – or are capable of building.

14. WHAT'S THE CATCH? . . . IT SOUNDS TOO GOOD TO BE TRUE . . .

Yes, there is a catch – *hard work and persistance*. Nothing more than that! . . . particularly for the first 100 days.

There is a very straight forward answer to every objection – real credibility lies in being able to provide it easily with both assurance and authority.

A few simple rules and pointers for dealing with objections:

1. 'Objections' are positive not negative. They are requests for information and therefore a display of real interest.

2. Develop a good technique using 'leading questions'. If you come up against an impasse, use the all-purpose question – 'that's interesting – why do you say that?'

3. Always 'bend with the wind' – don't get into an argument.

4. Be sympathetic – 'I know how you feel! I felt exactly the same until I found . . .'

5. Get people to expose their anxieties.

6. People will only reveal themselves at their own rate – don't push too hard. Sometimes you have to give before the other person can.

7. Get people to answer their own objections – that way most of them will, like smoke, be blown away and will, as a result, amount to very little.

8. Be patient, be understanding – and above all, remember how you felt when you first heard about Network Marketing.

PROSPECTING – LOOKING FOR GOLD

In the great old days of pioneering many brave souls set off, often into the most inhospitable wilderness, with their hearts set on the idea of getting rich. They were gold prospectors, men with a powerful dream, armed with little more than a pick and shovel and an inexhaustable supply of optimism. They knew that looking in the right places – places where the conditions suggested gold *might* be found – made more sense than simply looking *anywhere*. The odds were still long but a modicum of planning made a favourable difference.

In your search for gold through the medium of Network Marketing, you must prospect – and your prospects are *people*. Without prospects to approach, *your* prospects are negligible!

We are all surrounded by millions of people who have a need for our products – or would appreciate being offered the chance to earn extra income if they only knew how and where to start.

Prospecting must become a continuous process. It amounts to little more than simply *living in a community with your eyes and ears wide open*.

If you were to walk from one end of your home

town to the other, you would rub shoulders with hundreds, if not thousands of people. Our basic problem is getting any one of them into a face-to-face situation – in other words, creating the opportunity to present our plan or product. In your daily life opportunities to talk to people occur all the time quite naturally, particularly if you are a gregarious person. You should try to acquire the habit of exploiting these occasions – but never forget that all you are seeking from chance encounters is the opportunity of an appointment to give you the chance to make a presentation or sell the product or service.

In your role of retailer, you need prospects who will become your customers. But in your role as a wholesaler, you also need prospects who can see the benefits of becoming retailers. These two apparently different types of prospect may well turn out to be the same people. In seeking one you may well find the other, so your prospecting is always a double edged sword, and this dual purpose can add enormously to your chances of success. Those who buy from you may well become your eventual retailers, whilst those you attempt to recruit as retailers may simply end up as customers. This has got to make the whole business of prospecting a highly profitable and rewarding activity.

Your eventual success in this industry depends, as I keep stressing, on duplicating yourself and your effort, so it will be determined very much by your ability to prospect and seek the opportunity to show your business plan to a sufficient number of the right sort of people. The person who is a good and persistent prospector will build his organization swiftly and efficiently. I have never really liked referring to this business as a numbers game – yet, there is no escaping the fact that that is what it is – but never lose sight of the fact that it is primarily *a people game*. Simply seeing a sufficient number of people will ensure your success as a statistical certainty. Despite all the remarks about sharing, accept the fact that you *are* a salesperson – because you are selling an opportunity – but, unless you see a constant flow of people, on a regular basis, nothing much will happen.

It is a fact that, even though a salesman may not be very bright technically, if he sees a sufficient number of people, he *will* succeed. Even though it is a numbers game, always remember that you are dealing with warm-blooded human beings, just like you or me. Selling, whether it be ideas and concepts or products, is 98% people knowledge to 2% product knowledge!

Prospecting can be a lot of fun when you know you have two sure-fire things to offer – splendid products in which you believe and from which everyone can benefit, and an opportunity to either earn a bit more cash on a part time basis, or to start a serious business with unlimited potential.

So, where do you begin?

Let's start by dividing our field of operations into two main areas:

1. Your warm Market
2. The Cold Market

YOUR WARM MARKET is, without any doubt at all, the finest place to start prospecting in this new business of yours, to get things moving without delay. Your warm market embraces everyone you know, knows you, or has merely heard of you. You are amongst people with whom you have credibility, and most of the people in this category are people of whom you have some personal knowledge – not that that will necessarily be an advantage! It can sometimes be easier to talk to complete strangers.

Your warm market is made up of people to whom you have relatively easy access. The most powerful section of your warm market is certainly friends and relatives.

'Just a minute!' I hear your plaintive cry, 'I told you there was no way I was going to try and sell to my family and friends.'

Don't worry – nobody is suggesting you should! But what you must recognize is that these are the very people – *because they are your closest associates* – most likely to want to help you. There are probably 15 to 20 people you know fairly intimately who would *like to see you succeed* at this new venture upon which you have embarked. Let them *see* what you are doing. Let them monitor your progress. They are *vital* to your future development.

Go and see them; enlist their aid. Tell them what you are doing, let them see your enthusiasm and excitement, let them try your products and tell you what they think – but also let them know there is no way you are *asking* them to buy anything. All you are asking is that they refer you to *their friends* – people that you probably don't know. Get them to give you names, allow you to use their name by way of introduction.

Perhaps you are already beginning to see how important it is to understand human beings and what makes them tick. Multi-Level Marketing is very much a 'people business' where personal rapport is of vital importance.

Make a rule that you thank anyone who gave you a referred lead – not just at the time, but let them know the outcome of their introduction. People really do appreciate being thanked. Who knows, it might lead to a few more names or even acquiring that person as a customer. People feel good about being thanked just as they enjoy being asked for their help. One of the great keys to successful living is knowing how to make other people feel good about themselves. Achieve that and they will do anything for you.

Literally everyone you buy from in the course of daily life is a prospect. They are all people who may feel restricted in their earning power by the nature of their business. A source of additional income and the possibility of greater financial freedom may be a very attractive proposition. You will never know unless you ask! Very few people will reject the sincere offer of a chance to explore something which might be of serious benefit to them.

You may not be attempting to sell anything to your friends and family, but it would be churlish not to give them an idea of the business opportunity you intend to offer *their friends*. If you have something really worthwhile to offer, it is your friends you would wish to tell first, isn't it? If you are prepared to do favours for strangers, how much better to do favours for friends.

Approached carefully and sincerely, your warm market could produce a splendid supply of prospects to help get your business off the ground very quickly.

Do recognize the great value of the referred lead. It is quite easy to build a referral 'chain' by planting the seed of the idea quite early in the conversation with a new prospect: 'What I am going to tell you about may not actually appeal to *you* but very likely you will know people to whom it will appeal.' Having sown the seed and, by doing so, advertised the fact to your prospect that you are going to ask him for referred leads, he will be thinking of names even before you mention the matter again. Once the chain has started, and providing you are dedicated to getting leads as the easiest way of doing the job, sponsoring and building your down-line organization becomes a very straightforward business and is not at all difficult. If you find it easy to get referred leads, teach others the value of the idea as the best of all recruiting methods.

A referred prospect, unlike a cold prospect, is very easy to talk to. You both start from common ground – the person you know in common. In your place of work, leads can be generated quite naturally through working colleagues. But, take care; try to avoid being handed round within your company as you can easily die a death through over familiarity. You need both internal and external referrals to take you into a variety of other environments. Try asking the question; 'Do you know anyone who could do with some extra income?' It is such a simple and straight-forward question! Who could fail to give you an answer?

Divide your life into ten year periods and try to think of names from every age range of your life so far. You will be surprised at the resultant list. Think about people you know through clubs, organisations, trade unions, church, P.T.A. groups, parents of your children's friends, people from whom you buy – the possibilities are endless. And these are all people to whom you have relatively easy access.

THE COLD MARKET – everyone else!
The chances are that because you are looking at this business you are a somewhat gregarious and outgoing individual – a person who finds it easy and congenial to talk to strangers almost anywhere. If you have something exciting to tell people, it isn't very difficult to engineer the opportunity you need to speak to them, whether you know them or not! If they are not interested, it really doesn't matter – there are always plenty more. Too many people get worried by fear of rejection. If you make an approach to someone and they are not interested, *they are not rejecting YOU* – they are merely rejecting an idea. Get on to the next one – there are plenty of others who *will* see the value in your offer. As I suggested earlier, look on the

activity of prospecting as a statistical exercise – there is a predictable number of people who must say NO before one says YES! Think of it this way: if every person who said YES was worth £10 to you, and if only one person in every ten you approached *said* YES, *then each person you appraoch earns you £1 – whether they say YES or NO!* To some people that is a very comforting approach.

A prospect is simply *ANY PERSON to whom you can tell your story, explain your business and marketing plan (the opportunity) or to whom you can demonstrate the value of your product.* Don't judge people; you cannot make decisions for or about others. The most unlikely person might turn out to be one of your Aces – and the person you judged as a potential winner may drift away after a couple of months.

Your personal world is full of people who would appreciate your product or would welcome the opportunity to investigate the idea of earning extra income. They just need someone to come along and show them how to do it.

Prospecting is like breathing – *it must be a continuous process.* Approached in the right spirit – with determination, planning and optimism – *you can never run out of prospects.*

Surprisingly, some people develop a mental block over the idea of prospecting – it becomes something they actively dislike. It can sometimes become necessary to find ways of getting round this. Ask your reluctant associate which is worse – the anticipated distress of doing something you don't like doing, OR, *missing the rewards that will come from doing it*?

Try to get over any mental blocks you or any of your associates may have about prospecting – as we have already said, a NO in prospecting or selling is not a *rejection*. Point out to anyone having trouble over rejection that the 100% conversion rate is an impossibility! There *must* be people to say NO so that others can say YES!

In most selling situations a 50% conversion rate would be regarded as excellent – *but it still means that half the number of people approached HAVE SAID NO!*

To help your more reticent recruits get over call reluctance or fears of rejection, try a simple experiment – launch a competition, the object of which, to be the winner, is to achieve a score of 20 NO's *in succession*! Each time the contestants get a YES, they must start again! Don't tell the competitors that they are attempting something that they will probably find impossible – let them discover that for themselves.

Show me a person who will tell his story to four new people every day,, and I will show you someone destined for real success!

But, show me a person who cannot find enough people to tell his story to, and *there* is someone destined for failure.

THE REALITY

Have you ever worked for yourself before – particularly, have you ever had a home-based occupation?

It is not as simple as you might imagine – I have already mentioned the dangers of home as a 'comfort zone'.

If the experience of self-employment and of working from home is new to you, take heed, a lot of self-motivation will be needed. You are going to require both discipline and strong and vividly defined goals.

Being forewarned of the pitfalls might help you to avoid some of them without having to learn the hard way.

Don't initially involve yourself in a lot of expense by producing printed stationery and trying to set up a professional working environment until you have well and truly laid the foundations of your Network. Once the first 100 days are behind you, you can really consider yourself to be on your way – and all the evidence to back that up should be very evident.

By the end of that 100 days, you will have planted the seed-corn of your operation. The toe-in-the-water aspect of the development will be over and you should have acquired good working habits. You could *now* feel that some expenditure on image is justifiable.

Throughout the initial 100 DAYS plan, be prepared to work all the hours available to you. Stick to this and your success is virtually assured.

Get all the help and advice you can – and only listen to people who know what they are talking about. Keep away from negative people. Remember all the time that you are marketing two things – a splendid business opportunity and/or a very saleable product – which, handled correctly, dove-tail perfectly to produce a reciprocal win–win situation.

It is important to develop a feeling for timing; there is usually a right and a wrong time to approach a prospect. In just the same way, a decision on the appropriate approach has to be made – with one person it might be appropriate to present the product, with another, more advantageous to present the business opportunity. Either way you always have the other half of the package up your sleeve to produce when the time is appropriate and more opportune.

As we saw in the section on prospecting, you are involved with two basic markets and each presents its own particular problems:

THE COLD MARKET
Problems: 1. Time – researching for names etc.
2. Expense – mailshots, phone calls, travel etc.
3. No 'professional' base from which to work, to which you can invite strangers.
4. Communications skills – you may not feel sufficiently confident to put your

message across clearly and professionally.

THE WARM MARKET

Problems: 1. Knowledge – in the early stages you
may lack confidence and be worried
about your ability to answer all
questions.
2. Credibility – you may feel that you are
not always taken seriously by people
who know you well and know that you
are very new to Networking.
3. Friends and relatives – you may have a
reluctance to approach them – for both
the above reasons.
4. Procrastination – your own excuses for
not approaching the number of people
you should, possibly for fears of rejection or failure. Fear of starting on those
you know, for the same reasons.

It is a popular misconception that an abstract painter
probably cannot draw! Nothing could be further from
the truth. If he is any good, the likelihood is that he
has had just as fine a professional training as the purely
figurative painter – indeed he could not have reached
the creative level that abstract painting demands
without a thorough grounding in all the basic skills any
painter must acquire. In the world of Multi-Level and
Network Marketing, just as in the world of creative

141

art, there are also no short cuts that dispense with the need for knowledge, skill or activity.

Be sure that *you* are the master of everything I have discussed in this book and that you are capable of handling every aspect of the skills needed to allow you to build a successful Network. It really is necessary that you are conscientious about this and feel totally confident in talking to anyone.

However – and this could be the good news! – with some organizations operating Network Marketing schemes, *there are two possible short cuts* to help overcome many of those communication and knowledge problems listed above – but, like the abstract painter, neither absolves you from the need for acquiring all the skills you can.

Wouldn't it be splendid to have someone else do a great deal of the work for you in recruitment and sponsoring – or simply in putting across the concept of Network/Multi-Level Marketing? And, if you could be sure that all the people you want to approach were exposed to a thoroughly professional presentation – probably a good deal better than you could achieve – nothing but benefit would result. The simple answer is being prepared to invest in either books or videos.

VIDEOS

Several of the larger Networking organizations now use videos as a very practical approach to the recruitment process. Just think what that means in terms of time. By leaving videos for your prospects to view in their own time, your message – regarding both your product and the method of marketing employed for its distribution – can be passed to many people simultaneously, probably with a greater potential success rate than you might personally achieve. However, if you are involved with one of the companies that uses videos, please don't get the idea that this is the end of all the hard work, and that the video is going to achieve everything for you. *It is only intended to act as an introduction to YOU* – and what you represent. Once initial interest has been captured, it is still down to *you* to capitalize on the situation and get your prospect to attend an opportunity meeting.

The advantage of the video is that it can be the answer to many of the problems listed above. It can bypass the problems of:

1. **Knowledge** – it is accurate and informative – in a flawless presentation, endlessly repeatable.
2. **Credibility** – The video is totally professional. It is the video that will be judged – not you.
3. **Friends and relatives** – they are judging the video, not you. The video will add greatly to your credibility through the professional image it imparts.
4. **Procrastination** – discountable since all you have to do is send the video, asking your prospects to view it.

Many people in the Networking business now send videos out into the cold market too – usually preceded by a phone call or letter – with the hope that the statistics will do the rest.

Videos can represent a fast-track route to speedy development, handled sensibly. But remember, there is one golden rule in using this approach, just as with any other initial approach – *you must follow up every contact*. It may seem unnecessary to mention this but you might imagine that if the video is good, your prospective recruits will be sufficiently intrigued or excited to immediately contact you. Don't delude yourself! Occasionally this will happen, but, to maximize on the exercise, *you must follow through*. If you are a golfer, you know all about the importance of the follow-through in your golf swing. Without it you won't exactly miss the ball, but it certainly won't go very far!

BOOKS

As I have kept pointing out, you have two distinctly different things to sell – one is obviously your product, and the other is the concept of Network Marketing. I have also repeatedly mentioned those people wanting to come into this business just to earn a bit more immediate cash – people who wish nothing more than to simply retail the product. Such people will only be interested in the product and its sales potential. Retailers are always useful 'extras' to the system as they help to keep the products moving and your retail profits flowing whilst you are spending time in recruiting and sponsoring the really serious people.

In developing your network, it is the *concept* of Networking itself that is the most important message to get across to your prospects. That is the exciting and stimulating part of what you have on offer. *And this is where a good book can be of immense benefit.* If an explanatory book can be purchased in sufficient volume that its unit price makes it viable to send out as a prospecting tool, it can be of incalculable value as your ambassador. The object is to excite the imagination about *an idea*, even before your prospect knows anything about your product. If the product is presented enthusiastically *before* the concept, the unconscious emphasis is placed on selling – which can be a distinct disadvantage.

Since so many professional people are now coming into Network Marketing schemes, such a book must put its message across clearly, briefly and in an adult way that does not in any way trivialize the message of Networking/MLM. A good book will lay good foundations and save time in giving your prospect a sound understanding of Networking from the outset. I am simply reporting fact when I say that my own book, 'Network & Multi-Level Marketing', has already been used very successfully in this way because, such a book standardizes the approach and knowledge. In the constant repetition of a message, human beings can cut corners, often inadvertently, and, by so doing, dilute the message. A book keeps the message both fresh and complete.

Some people send the book out with a short explanatory letter – 'here is something you might find interesting' or something along those lines. Add that you will be in touch in a few days' time to get the prospect's view on what he or she has read. The most important lesson to learn at the outset, is not to give people very long before you make your second contact. The more time they think they have to read the book, the more they will put it off.

A more effective and intriguing approach is to send the book out with nothing – except one of those small self-adhesive labels stuck inside the front cover. Why not have this printed (such labels are amazingly cheap) with nothing more than your telephone number? Those that are excited by the content of the book may well contact you before you contact them – and that is a very powerful situation.

This, of course, will only happen occasionally, so, after you know they have had the book for two days, telephone your prospect and ask what they thought of it. If they tell you they haven't had the time to read it yet, don't be surprised – this is totally predictable, believe me! If the book is right for the job it should be possible to read it in a couple of hours at the very most, so there is little scope for procrastination on the grounds of not having time. An hour or two spent in reading something that might be instrumental in changing the course of one's life, could certainly not be described as time wasted. Don't reveal anything about your product but simply suggest that he or she try to make time to read the book in the next couple of days because before you say anything else you need to know if the concept the book explains is of interest. Add that, if it is not, you will collect the book as there are other people eager to read it.

If, on your next call, your prospect tells you he likes what he has read, let him keep the copy. It is then up to you to capitalize on the introduction the book has created for you.

A word of warning: don't send out too many books at a time. Pace your campaign to what you know you can reasonably handle. This is not such an expensive operation as it may sound since there will always be copies to collect and redistribute.

Keep accurate records so that follow-ups are made at the right time. Get the time scale wrong and all the energy will go out of the exercise and probably mean that you have wasted a lot of effort, time and money. So, don't send out large numbers – a dozen or so at a time on a regular basis should keep your prospecting on the move.

I have placed considerable emphasis on recruiting in fives as you develop your Network. The fives are the really serious people who see a future in Networking and are prepared to work as hard as you towards its realization. Never forget that *duplication* is the single most important feature of Network Marketing – and that is never achieved until the third level is in place. Only then does the immediate responsibility for the teaching/learning process move away from that person. Learn this and *teach this*:

Nothing is really secure until you have reproduced yourself.

Not everyone will agree over the idea of recruiting in fives. Many people favour the idea that strangth lies in width and not in depth. A little exercise in lateral thinking will show that, in a sense, one can achieve the best of all worlds by developing to, say, five or six levels in depth and then starting again with a new front-line five and promoting a whole new down-line. This way one could be said to be benefiting from both width and depth.

Sticking to five people is no more than keeping control in a very personal way in the hope of setting good examples and maintaining motivation through personal contact and involvement, at least through the first two levels.

THE THREE WAYS
OF EARNING

Network Marketing benefits from what is known sometimes as 'multi-plex' earnings. Most people, in their normal occupations are used to 'linear' earnings. With linear income you get a day's pay for a day's work. With the exception of certain very highly paid occupations, linear earnings will never accumulate great wealth.

There is a third method of earning known as 'residual' income. As the name implies, residual income comes through benefiting from sales initiated in the past, such as renewal commissions continuing from year to year on insurance policies, royalties on the sale of books and records etc.

Multi-plex income accrues through the actions of others, as in a manufacturing industry where independent wholesalers or distributors create the earnings of the manufacturer through their activity, but without being under the manufacturer's direct control. However, there is a subtle difference between the multi-plex income of a manufacturer and that of an operative in Network Marketing. The industrialist pays out vast sums of money for advertising and promotion, even before his product gets to the distributor. As we know, one of the great benefits of Networking is that advertising is done by word of mouth and by example, creating a far more immediate sales environment – and altogether, a far more profitable situation.

In the world of Network Marketing, earnings are derived from three main sources:

1. Retailing
2. Wholesaling
3. Networking

Let's take a closer look at each of these in turn.

1. RETAILING.

The people doing the retailing, and nothing more, are often those who see Network Marketing as a means of providing that bit of extra cash to boost the family budget without creating too much hard work. They are content with the profit they make in buying from a wholesaler and selling to their customers.

Retail profit, however, can mean different things to different people. As an individual develops a Network and the overall volume of their sales through that Network increases, so the rewards increase. The person who becomes a wholesaler (dealing *direct* with the manufacturer or supplier of a service) may benefit from say a 3% overriding commission on the total volume of sales achieved by his entire organization but, as that volume increases, the percentage profit paid on his own retail sales can increase too, through the medium of higher discounts on the price at which he buys from the manufacturer – these are given by way of rewarding him for the development he has created. Personal sales become even more attractive on this basis and provide the incentive for *everyone*, at any level, to generate at least *some* retail business of their own. One of the essential features of Networking is that large numbers of individuals are each selling relatively modest amounts of product. The product must obviously always be on the move or nobody gets paid!

2. WHOLESALING

The moment one individual in the Network supplies another individual (who is not the end user or customer) with the product, that person can be said to be wholesaling. It is the wholesaler that deals direct with the manufacturer, and in many companies he is known as a Direct Distributor. One of the fundamental features of Networking is that the wholesale price never varies – other than, of course, when general price rises occur. The rewards achieved by everyone in the chain of distribution, at varying levels of production, come in the form of rebates (discounts), profits and commissions.

3. NETWORKING

This third means of earning, as already mentioned above, is based on a bonus paid on the overall volume of business achieved through the entire Network developed by an individual. Many people have made the mistake, when looking at Network Marketing for the first time, of assuming that it is necessary to be in at the beginning to earn large rewards. Networking offers equal opportunity to everyone – indeed, I will stress again that it is one of the very few examples of real equal opportunity in business today. Each new entrant, the moment he/she starts work, is at the apex of their own development – and that can grow to any size. Clearly then the very high rewards that are the potential of Networking, are available to *anyone and everyone*, providing they bring the right attributes and attitudes to the enterprise.

Taking these multi-plex earnings into account, it is easy to see how, when sustained effort and determination are applied, a very interesting income pattern can be achieved – the only limitations are those the individual will impose upon him/herself. Clearly the aim *must be* to attain a level of Network development that attracts that vital volume bonus or override commission – usually about 3%. This bonus is the most important and significant factor in the earning pattern for anyone who intends to build an ambitious down-line development. *THAT*, in the long term, is what will provide the glittering prizes Networking is capable of producing – and 100 DAYS plan is designed to get you there with the least possible delay!

So, I repeat, you have the potential to earn:

　　1. Retail earnings on personal sales – the percentage or profit margin will vary depending on your position on the stepladder of achievement.

2. Wholesale earnings based on the volume of product passing through your hands as you supply others in your down-line development.

3. Networking earnings represented by that all-important percentage paid as an override on the entire production developed and stimulated by you.

In most jobs you are paid what the job is worth –
in Network Marketing you are paid WHAT YOU ARE WORTH!

THE SELLING –
building the retail side

Although we have talked a lot about the importance of building a strong and sound network through sponsoring and teaching others to sponsor, there is still one aspect of a good Network Marketing/MLM organization that we have not explored in any great detail, and that is building a retail side to your business.

As you will guess from everything I have so far said, it is not every Networking organization that will actively encourage the building of a retail business. Sponsorship and reliance on sharing the product is all that some organizations will suggest. Clearly, providing that sponsorship is a continuous process and all those who join use the products themselves, a considerable volume of goods is always on the move. The retail sales that this represents is likely, as a collective effort, to produce, for some, quite satisfactory results.

There are, of course, many people attracted to Networking who have no intention or wish to spend time sponsoring others or in building a network of their own. These are the people – the retailers or dealers – who might benefit most from this chapter.

Rule number one in selling anything at all must be

know your product. And its not just a question of knowing it, but having that familiarity with it that can only come through personal use. Know the product, use the product, believe in the product. The deeper your knowledge and appreciation of the product, the greater will be your enthusiasm in sharing (selling) it. It is easy to enthuse about something you know intimately – impossible if your knowledge is scant.

Enthusiasm is a fine spring-board but, developing some skill in selling is a great additional asset. If you are good at sponsoring, you are obviously already a good salesperson, because sponsoring is nothing more than selling an opportunity.

We have looked at the importance of belief in your product and we have discussed the effect enthusiasm can have on others so you may feel that if you are in possession of these two attributes, you *must* be a good salesman. *You might just be wrong*! Selling is a subtle process of advance and retreat, of giving and of taking away again, of knowing when to speak and when to listen.

How often have you heard people say – 'he's a born salesman! He really does have the gift of the gab'?

A born salesman? What on earth does that mean? Would you like to have your heart bypass done by a born surgeon? I'd only trust him if I was assured he was a *trained* surgeon. There is no such thing as a born anything – except a baby. And that is packed with potential, just waiting for life to develop it!

As for 'the gift of the gab' . . . *Telling is not selling*.

156

It doesn't matter how much you *tell* a prospect about your product or service, if he doesn't *want* it he won't buy it. All selling revolves around that innocent little word WANT – as we already saw in relation to getting people to an opportunity meeting.

You may of course feel you can make your prospective customer want a particular product by telling him about it. You could be wrong! You must be able to demonstrate to him or her that they have a *need* for your product or service – and don't imagine that this will easily be revealed by asking what they feel. People don't work like that . . .

There is a little problem known as 'sales resistance' which is built into all of us, and the moment we suspect someone is trying to sell us something, up it pops – and down comes the portcullis! Sales resistance is the prospective customer's natural state, worn like a suit of armour. And like a suit of armour, there will be weak points that can be penetrated. Selling is a game which has to be played by certain rules, and each participant should know his or her role.

Subtlety, an understanding of people and un-obtrusive persistence are the weapons of the sales-person.

The game is easy to play once you realize that it is a simple reactive response for a human being to throw up the barricades whenever an approaching salesman is sensed.

The prospect though, through long experience, knows the rules of engagement, and will at first appear quite co-operative. After all, if an appointment was sought, he or she did agree to allow you into their house or office – though possibly not without the odd remark such as: 'well don't think you're going to sell me anything!' The prospect knows perfectly well what you do and what the purpose of the appointment is! Don't be fooled by this seeming innocence – and don't be put off either. Play the game by the rules and watch closely for what are known as buying or closing signals. The first 'close', in making your sale has already happened . . . it was being granted an appointment!

Your part in the game now, having penetrated the initial defences, is to create a whole series of 'mini closes' by discovering what your prospect actually *needs*, relating that to your product, transforming his need into a *want* and then *allowing him to buy from you!* The way in which you score points in this game is by the number of times you can make him say 'yes'!

Doesn't this process suggest that there is a cycle of events taking place? In the world of selling the process we are exploring is known as 'the sales cycle'. It is well worth looking at because all selling, to be successful, will follow the pattern:

THE SALES CYCLE
Prospecting – identifying those you wish to contact
Securing an appointment
The appointment – establishing empathy
Fact and feeling finding
Establishing a need
Translating need into want

Presentation or demonstration of product
Close!
Taking the order
Getting referred leads
Maintaining ongoing contact and service

There is no real need for us to explore all these stages individually since we have already covered certain aspects earlier in this book – for example prospectng and approaches for getting appointments.

What exactly is meant by 'fact and feeling finding'? There are, quite simply, two types of questions that can be posed. Fact finding is asking straight forward questions, seeking purely practical information and establishing basics. 'What do you do for a living, Mr. Smith?' The answer is a *fact*. 'Do you enjoy it?' 'Do you think you're well paid?' 'Could you use some additional income?'

These are all '*feeling*' questions that will uncover attitudes, aspirations, hopes and dreams – vital clues to an individuals deeper feelings. One of the easiest ways of getting people to open up is to question the answers to fact-finding questions. 'That's interesting! – why do you say that?'

When it is important that you know as much about your prospect as possible, silence is a great ally. Having asked a question and listened to the answer, remain silent and go on looking at your prospect with interest. We all hate silences of this sort and the natural instinct is to want to break it – but it must not be *you* that breaks it! Your prospect will tell you much more by way of answer to your original question – the part he or she was witholding!

Fact-finding must never seem to be an inquisition. It should be easy, relaxed and conversational. The questions should only be aimed at providing a back-drop for your client against which you can begin to see him more clearly and begin to establish needs. Once a need is identified in your prospect's mind, you can move to the next phase of the cycle and begin to present some of the benefits your product or service can offer to best match your prospects needs.

Now that his need has been recognised and it is clear that your product can go a long way to satisfying it, *want* is only a question away.

And yet it is surprising how many sales are lost at this stage – all too often because the salesperson cannot bring themselves to ask the final question that would close the deal!

The sales process is like a series of steps – visualize it as a staircase. Each step is the same height and the upward climb is easy, step by step – until, suddenly, there is an insurmountable step, three times the height of any other confronting the salesperson. That is how the timorous salesman sees the arrival of an imminent close.

But it should never be like that! There have been hundreds of books written on how to close a sale – infallible methods all. There are seminars on the subject, videos, tapes – all proclaiming unique systems for the closing of a sale.

May I too claim the infallible method – the Allen

Carmichael method – tried and tested, and available to you absolutely free of charge. JUST ASK!

'Shall we make out the order?'
'Do you think that will do the job for you?'
'Which colour would you like?'
'Would you like me to order one for you?'
'Are you quite happy about that?'

The questions you *could* ask are endless. But the whole point is they *must* be asked *in exactly the same conversational tone* used throughout the entire interview. Nothing should be, or needs to be *different*, everything must be *relaxed* and easy.

Any number of sales have been lost because the salesman simply couldn't *ask* for the order. A potential customer can quite easily be frustrated because he is not being helped to come to the conclusion *he wants* when it is abundantly clear the time is right. JUST ASK!

'Perhaps you'd like to think it over for a few days?' the nervous salesman suggests limply. All the prospect's submerged instincts suddenly spring into action again as he seizes this proffered last straw – the chance to be let off the hook. *This is only an instinctive reaction which may not really be intended!* Everyone heaves great sighs of relief. The salesman departs revelling in the idea that he 'didn't lose that one' by having to ask the dangerous question! The prospect, after his departure, begins to wonder what the whole visit was really about and cannot quite understand why

161

he feels so frustrated. Over the next few days the salesman builds up his hopes again – until, by he time he contacts his prospect, the accumulation of all his anxiety comes flooding down the telephone. The customer's survival instincts are alerted yet again and he says he has thought it over, but no, *sorry*! And that last little word makes our foolish non-salesman feel good, because he thinks he has built a good relationship.

Rubbish! Everything has been wasted – time, planning, effort, *everything* – and it need never have happened.

There is a story about a man who wanted to cut his lawn but his mower was out of action. He decided to ask his neighbour if he could borrow his machine. On the way round to his neighbour's house he thought of every possible reason the man could give for not lending the mower.

He got more and more frustrated as he dreamed up increasingly complicated and bizarre objections until he arrived at the house, knocked and, when the neighbour opened the door, blurted out 'Oh, keep your bloody lawnmower!'

Another classic danger is the over-sell. It is vitally important to recognize when the sale has 'completed' – to be able to read the signals that show quite clearly that your prospect is ready to buy. The excitement of the moment has caused many a would-be salesman – who *did* spot all the signs – to go prattling on, in his natural excitement, ethusing and eulogizing over his product to the point where he has so bored his prospect, all possibility of the sale has been lost for ever.

Closing a sale is only like closing a door. On a door frame there is a simple piece of wood known, not surprisingly, as the doorstop. As the sales situation develops and moves towards an inevitable conclusion you are in effect slowly closing the door until, when you come to your 'close', the door is firmly against the stop. But without the doorstop there is no real close and it is all too easy to push the door open again – then the sale is lost.

I have made several mentions of 'buying signals' but you may be wondering just what they are, and how they are recognized? Think for a moment – what is the most obvious buying signal of all? Genuine and enthusiastic interest! We would all recognize that and, I hope, respond to it by immediately closing the sale, easily and naturally.

Once 'the rules of engagement' are understood, you will realize that the defence mechanism can function right up to the last moment! One of the classic buying signals can appear when the prospect, sometimes quite aggessively, throws a positive barrage of questions at the salesman. All that is actually being said is 'if you satisfy me on these points, you've got the sale'. Don't ever feel threatened by questions of this sort – they are certainly genuine requests for more information and represent the final stages of closing. But woebetide the salesman who cannot answer them!

His credibility stands or falls on the way he responds. The message is a simple one – *know your product*.

Salesmen are the world's greatest optimists. They will talk about 'losing a sale' rather than being truthful and admitting they did not actually *get* it! You cannot lose what you never had in the first place.

Your reputation depends on your image, your attitude and your professionalism – and if, on some specific occasion, you didn't get the sale for some reason, you *could* come away with something that may have far greater value – REFERRALS to other people – the penultimate item on our list that represents the sales cycle.

Referred leads are the life blood of prospecting – they can cut your work in half and double your rewards. The least you should ever come away with from any appointment is two or three names and the permission of your prospect to mention his or her name when approaching their friends. If you haven't already done so, do read the section on prospecting.

And so we come to the last item in the sales cycle – the thing that literally completes the circle. You have put in a great deal of effort to acquire many of your customers. If you wish to build a reasonable retail business as *a part* of your total Networking activity, never lose sight of the fact that the main reason why anyone should favour your services as opposed to buying through normal retail outlets, is the personal aspect of your business. The fact that you are prepared to visit people in their homes, discuss their requirements then finally deliver the goods to their door, is a great service. It should be developed and nurtured. Good record keeping is the key to good service. All your customers should be contacted on a regular basis. It is more than likely, if yours are consumer products, that you have replaced items on the normal shopping list. Your customer must never be allowed to run out of such products. It is all too easy, if you do not appear at the right intervals of time, for a customer to go back to their original source of supply. Some customers may telephone you to re-order, but don't rely on it. You are offering a service and will be expected to maintain it. A good record keeping system will ensure that nothing and no one is forgotten.

If you are selling a once-and-for-all product with no possibility of repeat business, don't overlook the possibility that the manufacturer of your product is quite likely to introduce something new at some time in the future. Keep contact with your customers, develop good relationships – you never know when you might want to go back with a new product.

I have lectured many new recruits on entering a sales organization and there was one thing I always tried to make clear to them. The ideas and techniques that one can teach or suggest to ensure the successful conclusion of a sale must sometimes look to the newcomer very like manipulation. They are not! There is a world of difference between the words 'manipulation' and 'motivation'. Most selling techniques are based on a sound psychological knowledge of the way people think and respond under certain circumstances and in certain situations. I have mentioned selling as a 'game' and talked of the 'rules of engagement'.

These expressions are not meant to be flippant – they are designed to help you understand the psychology of the sales situation. It is only through this understanding that one is able to motivate a prospective customer towards a sale – beneficial to both parties – as easily and painlessly as possible. Everyone has the choice to say NO as a final and conclusive move. Motivation is often needed to help a person to come to a conclusion over something they would like to do – it is providing that little 'push'.

I would finally add one thought. If you are developing your MLM or Networking operation in the most profitable way, the bulk of your retail customers will have developed through your attempts at sponsorship – and conversely, many of your sponsorships will be people who started as retail customers. That double-edged sword again!

MAINTAINING THE STANDARDS – DELEGATING

It is never a bad idea, once in a while, to stop for a moment and remind yourself of what your original intentions were when you first started your enterprise. You most probably had bright ideals and strongly held concepts that you took as the basis for your business.

The question now is, how far have you strayed or deviated from those ideals? Have you unconsciously cut any corners? It is all too easy for an ideal to become slightly eroded or flawed – quite unintentionally and almost unnoticed – so, from time to time, do a stock-take and make adjustements and administer any fine-tuning that may be needed to set your ship back on an accurate course. When talking to people considering joining the network, remember what it felt like when you were in that very same position. Putting yourself in the other person's shoes can be no bad thing from time to time.

In the building of a large network, delegation – the sharing of authority – is something you must aim to develop. Split down large groups into smaller groups with a good person in charge of each. By delegation you are demonstrating confidence and showing trust in the people in whom you have belief.

Delegation needs *boldness* and a generosity of spirit. Never worry that a person may become better than you – if they were all better than you *YOU* would be a millionaire! Be generous in your delegation and use it to show people how much you appreciate their efforts. If you give most people their heads I guarantee they will surprise you. But take special care to see that you never tread on the toes of those to whom you have delegated authority. What might have been intended as help and encouragement could be construed as interference and lack of confidence.

Delegation, to some, is not an easy thing to achieve. There are people who like to give the impression of being over-worked. Delegation is not for them. There are others who cannot or will not let go as they have a fear that they may be seen as dispensable. And there are always those – and there are many of them – who think it is quicker to do a job themselves than waste time explaining it to others. At this point I think it would be a good idea to lay down a few ground rules:

1. Decide what you could delegate – *and write it down*.

2. Decide who is capable and has the energy, drive and interest to carry the job through.

3. Decide that you *are* willing to relinquish authority whilst retaining responsibility. Never give away both authority and responsibility – this way you merely diminish your own stature and lose respect.

4. Show people you trust them. Only tell them *what* you want them to do – let them decide *how* they will set about doing it.

5. Be prepared to invest in time in teaching those to whom you are delegating. Monitor their progress so that you may correct or praise, as the case may be.

6. Realize the immense value of recognition and, if appropriate, reward. There is great value in touching a person as you praise them, even if it is simply a hand laid casually on a shoulder!

7. Publically praise, privately reprimand.

8. Never delegate tasks that others might perceive as your particular responsibility. This is guaranteed to cause resentment and do damage to your image.

Remember that new people have a great need for 'example'. They feel insecure, are very conscious of their lack of knowledge, and need to see how the job is done by those they perceive as successful. Always be very precise in your instructions to others so they can act easily and without confusion. For example, don't just tell someone to sponsor more people. Turn it into a challenge, make a goal of it – 'Let's see if you can sponsor 10 more people by the end of the year'.

Never withdraw your support from anyone until you have taught them to be supportive to others – then, and only then, is the time they no longer need to lean on you.

You cannot ever know the answers to all the questions you may be asked.

It is a far greater asset to know where information is available than to try and know it all yourself.

If you always do a good job yourself you will leave people feeling better for their association with you – and that will have a very beneficial effect on you too! If you can walk away from a situation feeling you have been of benefit to someone else – and you know you have done a good job – you will have brought enrichment to the lives and experience of two people.

THE LAW, SAFEGUARDS & ETHICS

As we have already seen, Pyramid Selling was outlawed by legislation because for its success it relied on both unethical and unscrupulous practices. There were many honest people, who, believing they were involved in a genuine opportunity, were exploited by the ruthless few.

The law put an end to marketing schemes that were based on the idea of the ever-increasing wholesale price of a product as it passed downwards through a number of 'levels' before reaching the consumer – if, indeed, it ever did. Many people suffered financially, being caught out holding large stocks of goods which were vitually unsaleable – over-priced to the extent that they had no possible market. The media quite rightly exposed these schemes, and stories of wrecked lives abounded in the popular press.

There is still a stigma attached to anything that looks remotely like Pyramid Selling *as it was known*. It is now left to the industry to find its own way of getting over this legacy, this tarnished image – and there is only one real answer to this problem, namely, to promote an image that is totally beyond reproach.

There are two instruments of legislation that now control and legalize all MLM and Network operations. These are:

The Pyramid Selling Schemes Regulations 1989 (No. 2195)
The Pyramid Selling Schemes (Amendment) Regulations 1990 (No. 150)

Copies of both the above documents are obtainable from:

H.M. Stationery Office,
P.O. Box No. 276,
London SW8 5DT
Telephone No. 071 873 9090

Perhaps, rather than wade through all the legal jargon of 'Statutory Instruments' you might prefer a very straight-forward precis of the law relating to these matters. The D.T.I. – Department of Trade and Industry – produce an excellent pamphlet which summarizes all the main legislative points very adequately. The name of this document is: 'Multi-Level Selling Schemes. A guide to the Pyramid Selling Schemes Legislation' and it may be obtained from:

The Department of Trade and Industry,
Consumer Affairs Division 3,
10–18 Victoria Street,
London SW1H 0NN
Telephone No. 071 215 3344

NOTE: I would just like to make a personal observation here. It would be so helpful if the words 'Pyramid Selling' could be dropped from the title to this publication. I realise that it is not possible to alter the title to a Parliamentary instrument, but changing the title of the D.T.I. booklet to, say . . . 'Multi-Level Selling Schemes. A guide to the controlling legislation,' would be both helpful and diplomatic! The perpetuation of those two words still causes so much unnecessary trouble and gives rise to so many long-winded explanations as to what Network marketing *is not.* Many people have never heard of Multi Level Marketing or Network Marketing, yet, almost without exception, these same people have heard of Pyramid Selling – and, of course, always in a detrimental way. The perpetual linking of all these titles really helps nobody but certainly confuses many.

A legal contract under the 1989 regulations requires that certain requirements are met, namely:

1. The date on which a MLM programme started in the U.K. – or, if it is in a pre-launch phase, the date on which it is intended to start must be shown.

2. The name and address of the promoters must be made known – and this includes all promoters, should there be more than one.

3. A description of the goods or services being promoted or offered through the operation.

4. The legal capacity of the members of the programme.

5. A Statutory Warning must be prominently

173

displayed in the contract – and there are very detailed requirements regarding exact size and precise placement of this information.

6. Information regarding the rights of participants 'in connection with termination . . .'

I must emphasize that the six items listed above only skim the surface of the 1989 Regulations. For more detailed information you should examine the document for yourself, not forgetting the new Regulations that came into force in March 1990. Suffice it to say that the legalities though complex are reasonably comprehensive, yet still leaving – as many such documents do – a number of issues very much open to personal interpretation.

If you are considering joining a MLM operation, common sense should dictate the safeguards with which you should acquaint yourself. Do not allow yourself to be hurried into anything. Any opportunity that is worthwhile will still be there in a few days time, no matter what you are told about 'getting in on the ground floor'. Anyone offering you an opportunity to join their scheme is not going to tell you about all the other possibilities. Take your time, look around – because it is so important that you only join a scheme that really means something to *you*, either from the point of view of its product(s) or because you feel a particular empathy towards the people involved.

Do not part with any money until you are totally confident that you have been provided with all the information you need to assess the worth of the operation, the product, and the opportunity – and have a realistic idea of your expectations for the future. Judge a company – as you would an individual – on how it presents itself and its product.

What is its reputation and standing?
Has the product credibility, value and quality?
Decide whether you would find it easy to sell
– and is there a market for it in your area?
Is the price of the product competitive?
Is the product repeatable – to offer ongoing sales?
Is the product unique, or . . .
can anything similar be bought in local stores?
Does the wholesale/retail price ratio offer a realistic profit?
Does the organization provide adequate training to enable you
to maximize your opportunity?
Is there a charge for training and is it an on-going facility?
Does the company own the exclusive rights to the product?

These are all questions you should seriously address for your own security and satisfaction so that you can approach the opportunity you are being offered with both confidence and a true expectation of realistic rewards.

The Regulations provide protection for the individual and have rid the industry of the unacceptable practices that beset it. It is, in my opinion, the duty of everyone working in the MLM and Network Marketing world to strive to produce a whiter-than-white image. We must provide the industry not only with the right image, but also the necessary degree of respectability needed to carry it forward as an ever-expanding method of distributing goods and services to the ultimate benefit of the maximum number of people and without exploiting anyone.

EPILOGUE

THE CHOICE IS YOURS – THE CONCLUSION IS MINE!

Once you have made your decision to enter the fascinating world of Multi-Level or Network Marketing, unless you have already been sponsored into one particular organization, you could find that you are faced with a bewildering number of possibilitites.

Almost every day my post contains news of some new enterprise starting up offering a 'green-field' opportunity, the 'greatest-opportunity-of-a-lifetime', the 'once-and-for-all chance to achieve financial independence', each new operation purporting to be better than anything that has preceded it!

One of the startling factors of all these chances to become a millionaire is that the requirements appear to become less and less demanding! No selling, no recruiting, no stock to purchase and yet, the glittering prizes are still offered in abundance! This to me simply doesn't add up!

The book you are holding has taken quite some time to compile and the information and instruction it contains is, I believe, essential to the achievement of any real and lasting success in the field of MLM or Network Marketing. *I ask you to believe that the real rewards will only come as the result of following all the principles I have suggested*. If anybody tells you there are short cuts, or that success can be bought, I suggest you seriously question your adviser and his motives.

If you want to think it is possible to achieve financial independence without having to do anything, that is your decision – and I would appreciate a postcard from you when you feel you have done it!

As everyone knows, a few dubious individuals will always be attracted to any situation where the potential rewards are very high. Network Marketing is no exception. Please believe me when I say that the majority of people who have become seriously and significantly rich in Network Marketing, have done so *with the companies that retail products of undoubted quality, promote their business in a thoroughly ethical manner and encourage the concept of regular sponsorship*.

It is of course possible, as we have seen, to be involved in a number of MLM situations at the same time. I have never believed this to be necessary.

Nevertheless, there are people who like to hedge their bets, although the danger is always that they may be simply dissipating their energies and thereby diluting their eventual rewards. If you are determined to follow that course, the least I can do is to provide a few useful pointers to questions worth asking:

1. Are the products of the various companies with which you are involved, compatible to the point that they would appeal to the same public – the public, that is, you are approaching, and the clientele you have developed?

2. Do the operating and administrative systems dove-tail easily so as to keep your record-keeping simple and straight forward?

3. Are meetings involved with any or all of the Networking schemes with which you are associated?

4. Can you devote sufficient time to each enterprise to really make it work for you?

5. If your Networking involvement is only part time, do you have sufficient spare time to carry out your obligations to several operations?

6. From your experience of life generally, how well have you coped when you have had to handle a lot of things at the same time? Or, are you better when you channel all your attention in one direction?

7. From your experience as a consumer, have you noticed that it becomes progressively more difficult to make up your mind as the range of choice increases?

In making a choice initially, look at the opportunity with the greatest long-term potential. Consider the attitude and philosophy, so far as you can judge it, of the manufacturer. Look at the products and ask yourself whether they have an on-going potential or are you simply looking at a gimmick with a limited life? Find out how long it should take the average Distributor/Wholesaler to reach a realistic income level. And, of course, look at the people involved. Are they people and do they portray attitudes with whom and with which you would be happy to associate?

If there is a key to success in MLM it is simply to learn everything you possibly can about the principles of this system of marketing and only then to seek out the company and product you can truly believe in – and by joining it you have then a most powerful combination.

All the above points deserve serious thought and consideration. What I really want you to understand, though, is that *it only takes ONE good Networking/ MLM operation to make you rich!* – providing you believe in it and can give it sufficient time and attention. One of the main purposes of this book has been to preach this simple message and I do hope you don't feel I have been too over-emphatic in putting it across. Your success will be related absolutely to your commitment. If your commitment is of a sufficiently high order, you are bound to succeed so long as you *stick at it* for at least 3 months. If you have given it all you've got, and the results are not beginning to look very interesting at the end of that period, I would suggest Networking is not for you!

I am quite sure there are many people who are involved in quite a number of operations simultaneously who have no complaints whatsoever. They have a reasonable level of monthly income – everyone has his own particular comfort zone – but, depending on the nature of the opportunities they have joined, they could also have a considerable number of monthly outgoings – commitments to purchase goods for which they may have little or no use, other than that the obligation is there to purchase them as a means of earning commissions. There is something stultifying in a situation like this! Where does the excitement or

180

challenge lie? – perhaps just in the perpetual hunt for brighter and better opportunities, in the search for the goose which will lay the golden eggs!

You can only really decide for yourself and be guided by your own experience as it develops. Initially though, it makes sense to go for the experienced operation that has good products and demonstrates good attitudes to which you can easily relate. Strike the right balance between retailing, wholesaling and sponsoring, always remembering what the magic of multiplication can do for you. If you do things the right way, believe in yourself and your own ability and bring the right attitude and commitment to it you *will* discover that wondrous goose that lays those golden eggs – IT WILL BE YOU!

'This above all, to thine own self be true and it will follow, as the night the day, thou canst not then be false to any man.'

William Shakespeare.

GOOD LUCK!

REGISTRATION FORM (SS)

To: Concept
    P.O. Box 614
    Polegate, East Sussex
    BN26 5SS

Please add my name to your mailing list and send me news and information about future CONCEPT publications.

Title: Mr Mrs Miss _____

Forenames: _____

Surname: _____

Address: _____

_____

_____

Telephone number: _____

It would be helpful to know where you purchased this book:

_____

ORDER FORM (SS)

To: Concept
P.O. Box 614
Polegate, East Sussex
BN26 5SS. Telephone: 0323 485434

Please send me ...... copies of 'THE NETWORK MARKETING SELF-STARTER' @ £6.95 per copy plus .60p P&P (Total £7.55)

Please send me .... copies of 'NETWORK & MULTI-LEVEL MARKETING' By Allen Carmichael @ £4.99 per copy plus 53p per copy P&P (Total £5.52)

I enclose my cheque/postal order for £ ......

Name: ....

Address: ....

....

....

Postcode: ....

Telephone number: ....

I would be helpful to know where you purchased this book:

....

We are pleased to give substantial discounts for bulk orders, the percentage depending on number of copies required. Please telephone for details or complete this form without sending money, and we will contact you promptly.

NOTES

NOTES

NOTES